MARKET STREET

Xiao Hong and Xiao Jun (Langhua)

MARKET STREET
A Chinese Woman in Harbin

XIAO HONG

Translated with an Introduction by
HOWARD GOLDBLATT

UNIVERSITY OF WASHINGTON PRESS
Seattle and London

Library of Congress Cataloging-in-Publication Data
Hsiao, Hung, 1911-1942.
  Market street.

  Translation of: Shang shih chieh.
  Bibliography: p.
  I. Goldblatt, Howard, 1939-   . II. Title.
PL2740.N3S4513 1985   895.1'35   [B]   85-40357
ISBN 0-295-96266-6

Acknowledgments

THE following friends and colleagues read all or part of this translation, in one form or another, sharing with me their interpretations and opinions, keeping me properly humbled with their criticisms, and occasionally intoxicating me with their praise: Tani Barlow, George Cheng, Ruth Keen, Gretchen Swanzey, Noric Taschian, Brenda Webster, Roger Williams, and Ellen Yeung, as well as two anonymous readers engaged by the Press. I thank them, one and all.

Contents

Translator's Introduction

I should not talk so much about myself if there were anybody else whom I knew as well.
—HENRY DAVID THOREAU, *Walden*

"The only thing we *can* do," said Banaka, "is to give an account of our own selves. Anything else is an abuse of power. Anything else is a lie."
—MILAN KUNDERA, *The Book of Laughter and Forgetting*

AUTOBIOGRAPHY AND FICTION—the boundaries shift, grow hazy, merge, and separate. We are all, of course, giving an "account of our own selves" whenever we write, whenever we speak, whenever we act. Yet as readers we have a feeling that autobiography, however indefinably, differs from other "accounts." It is both more and less revealing of its creator, and it belongs simultaneously to the realms of conscious manipulation and subconscious exposition. It presents the author's life story, in part or in whole, as a search for personal identity, a means of self-justification or self-aggrandizement, or a complement to other personal endeavors, including creative writing. This reworking of one's own significance, this "sincere project of recapturing and understanding one's own life,"[1] distinguishes autobiography from the novel. A novelist, in writing his or her autobiography, gives an account of the self not only as an individual living in the world but also as a creative writer. What may be termed an artistic (or imaginative)

1. Philippe Lejeune, "L'Autobiographie en France," quoted in Avrom Fleishman, *Figures of Autobiography* (Berkeley, Los Angeles, and London: University of California Press, 1983), p. 17.

autobiography, therefore, attains that status partly as a result of the author's linguistic and structural sophistication, and partly through his or her application of literary techniques and devices used in the creation of fiction.

Market Street [Shangshi jie] is a work that could be (and has been) mistaken for a series of autobiographical essays or for a piece of fiction. It is, however, the story of the author's life during a specific period of time. It is thinly disguised as fiction (as in the use of pseudonyms for the narrator and her lover), and suggests a fictional style, owing to the selection and ordering of materials and the nature of the telling. Yet, given the known "facts" of Xiao Hong's life, including statements by contemporaries who figured prominently, both in her life and in *Market Street*, compelling reasons exist for accepting the work neither as fiction nor as a casual collection of related essays but as a coherent autobiography, a unified and precisely ordered set of motifs from the author's personal experience. It is also representative of women's autobiography in the main and gives clear and effective expression to Xiao Hong's world view, largely insofar as issues of gender are concerned. It is both feminine and feminist.[2]

Published a mere eight months after the appearance of Xiao Hong's first novel, *The Field of Life and Death* (Shengsi chang), *Market Street* gives an account of the narrator's life in Harbin, a city in Northeast China (Manchuria), from the summer of 1932 until sometime in May of 1934. This was a time of relative security and stability for Xiao Hong, who, in the two or three preceding years, had suffered more emotional and physical pain and degradation than many people have experienced in a lifetime.

2. I have dealt with this work in detail in my essay "Life as Art: Xiao Hong and Autobiography," in *Woman and Literature in China*, ed. Anna Gerstlacher *et al.* (Bochum, West Germany: 1985), pp. 345–63.

Xiao Hong (Hsiao Hung), whose real name was Zhang Naiying, was born on June 2, 1911, into a land-owning family in the town of Hulan, some thirty kilometers northeast of Harbin. She did not have an easy time in her father's house. Her childhood experiences and relationships were never far from her mind, as she made clear in the following autobiographical sketch, written in 1937:

I was born in 1911 in a small county seat into the family of a minor landlord. That city is probably the easternmost and northernmost county seat in China—in Heilongjiang province—so there are snow flurries for at least four months of the year.

Father often gave up his humanity over his own covetousness. His relationships with servants, or with his own children, as well as with my grandfather were all characterized by his stinginess, aloofness, and even hard-heartedness.

Once, over a delinquent rent payment on a house, Father took possession of a tenant's entire team of horses as well as his wagon. The tenant's family wept, pleaded, and threw themselves at Granddad's feet, who then unharnessed two tawny horses from the wagon and gave them back to them.

Father quarrelled with Granddad all night long over those horses. "Two horses mean nothing to us, but to a poor man they can mean his very existence," Granddad said, but Father continued quarrelling with him.

When I was nine my mother died, after which Father's idiosyncracies became even more pronounced: when someone broke a glass, Father would shout and carry on until the person shook in his boots. Afterwards, it seemed as though his glance could take in everything around him, and at such times, whenever I passed by him I felt as though my body were covered with thorns. He would cast an oblique glance at me, as that arrogant look of his shifted from the bridge of his nose, down past the corner of his mouth, and continued moving down.

So at dusk during snowstorms I stayed near the heater and by my grandfather, where I listened to him reading poetry and watched his slightly reddened lips as he read the poems.

Whenever Father beat me, I went to Granddad's room and stared out the window from dusk to late into the night.

Granddad often placed his two wrinkled hands on my shoulders, then on my head, and my ears rang with sounds of: "Hurry and grow up! It will be fine once you have grown up."

The year I reached the age of twenty I fled from the home of my father, and I have lived the life of a drifter ever since.

I've "grown up," all right, but things are not "fine."

Yet I learned from my grandfather that besides coldness and hatred, life also includes warmth and love.

And so, for me there is a perpetual longing and pursuit to find this warmth and love.[3]

Xiao Hong first arrived in Harbin as a teenager, when she entered the city's First Municipal Girls' Middle School. Her education was interrupted two years later, in 1930, when her father informed her that he had arranged for her marriage to the son of a local warlord and was taking her out of school. It was then that she "fled from the home of [her] father" and began living "the life of a drifter." She immediately moved in with a young intellectual whom she had met earlier in Harbin; he subsequently took her with him to Peking, where he ultimately abandoned her. She returned to Harbin alone, penniless, and pregnant in the fall of 1931.

Over the next several months Xiao Hong ate whatever she could beg and slept wherever she could find shelter (in a city where the temperature sometimes falls to −50° Fahrenheit!). Eventually she sought refuge in a small hotel run by a White Russian; there she became a virtual prisoner, in poor health and on the verge of total despair. A letter sent to a local newspaper led to her rescue from the hotel as the swollen Sungari River threatened to flood the city and as her pregnancy neared its term. Her brash young "liberator" was an aspiring writer named Xiao Jun (the Langhua of *Market*

---

3. Written at the request of Edgar Snow for a planned anthology of contemporary stories in English translation, published in *Baogao* (Shanghai: 1937), I: 1.

Street), with whom she began cohabiting in the summer of 1932, following the birth and adoption of her child. The account of their lives together in *Market Street* begins at this point. It ends as Xiao Hong and Xiao Jun take leave of Harbin to travel to the city of Qingdao (Tsingtao) on the Shandong Peninsula.

Harbin

Prior to the end of World War II, Harbin was nearly always a "foreign" city. Culturally dominated by Russian émigrés, and subsequently occupied by the Japanese, the city still shows traces of its unique, non-Chinese past. A contemporary of Xiao Hong, a Russian who spent much of his childhood in Harbin, has described it in the following terms:

> Harbin had been a small fishing village on the Sungari (Songhuajiang) in the early 1890's. Construction in 1897–1904 by Tsarist Russia of the Chinese Eastern Railway had transformed it into a town with a population of several hundred thousand. The town was divided into three sections: *Pristan* (Russian for Pier or Embankment); *Novi Gorod* (New Town) which adjoined it; and the native district, farther inland.
>
> *Pristan* and *Novi Gorod* together were the part that had earned for Harbin the name Paris of the Orient. The population was predominantly Russian; those who had left Russia before the October Revolution and, later, exiles cast out by the Revolution. There must have been around a hundred thousand of these, many of them workers and employees of the Chinese Eastern Railway. The Russians spoke no Chinese and showed no desire to master the language; the Chinese living in this part had to learn Russian, and some of them spoke it quite fluently and idiomatically. Even the rickshaw pullers, peddlers, shop assistants and barbers spoke Russian, though mercilessly distorted and mispronounced. All the stop signs were in Russian. The architecture was Russian. The whole tenor of life was Russian. And to cap it all, the main street was named *Kitayskayo*—China Street!
>
> A Soviet of Workers' Deputies and a Soviet of Soldiers' De-

puties had been set up here in March 1917, but were suppressed in December of the same year by the White Russians in collaboration with the troops of the Chinese warlords. By the time we moved here around 1918, the town was wholly "white", and getting "whiter" and "whiter" with the influx of ex-generals and admirals, bereft of their armies and fleets, ex-dukes and barons, deprived of their dukedom and baronies, ex-millionaires and near-millionaires, dispossessed of their millions.

But Harbin had its Parisian reputation to uphold. There was no place in its life for anything but gaiety.[4]

In September 1931, the Japanese attacked the Manchurian city of Mukden (Shenyang, in Liaoning province, south of Heilongjiang). Six months later, they formally annexed all of Northeast China. Xiao Hong and Xiao Jun thus began their lives together (their union, stormy from the start, would end six years later in the North China city of Xi'an) in a city under Russian influence and Japanese control. The latter circumstance drove them from Harbin and turned them into "anti-Japanese" writers with national reputations.

Xiao Hong never returned to her homeland. Arriving in Shanghai in 1934, she joined the circle of writers around Lu Xun and became a frequent visitor in the home of this most famous and influential modern Chinese literary figure. She subsequently spent time in Japan (less than a year), Wuhan, Xi'an, and Chongqing (Chungking). She died in Hong Kong of a respiratory ailment. The date was January 22, 1942, less than a month after the British colony had been militarily occupied by the Japanese with the start of World War II. She was thirty years old.

4. Sam Ginsbourg, *My First Sixty Years in China* (Beijing: New World Press, 1982, pp. 5–7.

Parts of Xiao Hong's autobiography were published in Harbin and Shanghai magazines as early as 1934. As *Market Street*, it was published in book form in August 1936 by the Shanghai Culture and Life Publishing Company, while Xiao Hong was visiting in Japan for reasons of poor health and a deteriorating relationship with Xiao Jun. The author's name on the cover was Qiao Yin, Xiao Hong's first pseudonym and also the name of the protagonist in *Market Street*. This pseudonym also appeared in 1933 on the cover of "The Book" in Chapter 29 (*Bashe* or *Trudging*), which was republished in Harbin in 1979. *Market Street* was initially well received and went to a second printing within a month. Since then, however, it has been neglected in China (it is the only one of her books that has not been reprinted in its entirety). Partly because the work is so unlike other autobiographies published there, it has been mistakenly perceived as autobiographical fiction. It thereby suffers in comparison with *Tales of Hulan River* (1940), Xiao Hong's superb autobiographical novel, set in her childhood home.[5]

In terms of character, technique, and theme, *Tales of Hulan River*, while unquestionably autobiographical, is, like Virginia Woolf's *To the Lighthouse*, decidedly fictional. It is a novel. *Market Street*, on the other hand, is autobiography; it is an anecdotal, imaginative recreation of the author's life during her final years in Harbin. Like Sylvia Plath's *The Bell Jar*, *Market Street* conveys thematic overtones beyond the explicit adventures experienced by the narrator/protagonist. The

---

5. My English translation (Indiana University Press, 1979) will be reissued in paperback in 1986 by Joint Publishing Company, Hong Kong.

reader will find only oblique references to the major historical events of the time, no systematic evocation of the author's life prior to the period covered, and a paucity of the dated material that one generally expects to find in autobiography. Clues to the past are given, but only when they have psychological import. Xiao Hong has selected and described a series of incidents (mainly minor), has recalled impressions, has reconstructed actual or created imaginary dialogue, and has interpreted events, behavior, and attitudes in retrospect. The work is episodic—framed in a generally linear format, but discontinuous in its detailed organization. Since it focuses entirely on a period that preceded the blossoming of her writing career, the author/narrator is revealed as an ordinary woman in ordinary circumstances. Xiao Hong has, to use Georges Gusdorf's words, "reassembled the scattered elements of [her] individual life and [has regrouped] them in a comprehensive sketch."[6]

In Xiao Hong's quest for "recapturing and understanding [her] own life" (it is significant that so many chapters end on unresolved issues or with unanswered philosophical questions), we are drawn both to the time frame of the story told and to the time of its telling, the latter for its interpretive insights. Nowhere is this more revealing than in the descriptions of the protagonist's lover and of their relationship. Although Langhua assumes a role as a dominant and positive character, who is forgiven his excesses and shortcomings by the self-demeaning narrator, the final impression, created by the author's selection of incidents and her suggestion of patterns, is decidedly negative. The work has a clear anti-male tone.

Market Street shares several characteristics with women's autobiography: a downplaying of the nar-

6. Georges Gusdorf, "Conditions and Limits of Autobiography," in James Olney, ed., *Autobiography: Essays Theoretical and Critical* (Princeton: Princeton University Press, 1980), p. 35.

rator/protagonist's own achievements, an emphasis on private rather than public roles, a heavy reliance on anecdote (which captures character at its most typical), and a discontinuous narrative style. Simultaneously, these characteristics invest *Market Street* with the literariness of Xiao Hong's novels and short stories. As a work of literature, *Market Street* rivals many of the most compelling creations of this and other periods of Chinese history in terms of its evocative power, universal accessibility, and rhetorical skill. As autobiography, it reveals the life *and* the general world view of a representative Chinese intellectual, a woman living in a male-oriented and male-dominated society in the chaotic period just prior to World War II. It describes a young woman's attempt to come to grips with the realities of her own life, thereby legitimizing her past to understand her present. *Market Street* is, in sum, literary autobiography at its finest.

MARKET STREET

1

The Europa Hotel

SUCH a long flight of stairs, like a pathway to the stars. Actually we had only a three-story climb, but I was walking on shaky legs that would no longer do my bidding; I grasped tightly onto the bannister and forced myself to keep going. After a few steps, my hand was trembling almost as violently as my legs.

When I finally made it into the room, I crawled into bed like a humiliated child and wiped my face with my sleeve.

He—my lover Langhua (he was still my lover then)—asked me, "You crying?"

"What makes you think I'm crying? It's sweat, not tears!"

Only after several moments did I realize how white the room was. It had a slanted ceiling and was furnished simply with a bed, a table, and a rattan chair. The table and chair were no more than two paces from the edge of the bed. Nothing could have been easier than opening the door: I needed only to reach from where I lay on the bed and push it open with my hand. Staying in this tiny white room would be like living inside a tent. My throat was parched.

"I ought to drink some water," I said.

He became so flustered in his desire to get me some water that his eyebrows creased into an almost unbroken straight line. His nose twitched several times.

"How're you going to drink it? What'll you drink from?"

The table was covered by a freshly laundered tablecloth and nothing else—not even a speck of dust.

I lay on the bed feeling light-headed. I could hear him talking to the hotel attendant out in the corridor;

3

then I heard the door close. As he walked up to the bed I assumed that he was holding a glass in his hand. But no, his hands were empty.

"What can you drink from? How about using the small wash basin?"

He picked up the newly bought wash basin from the rattan chair. Within it, under the facecloth, he discovered a toothbrush mug. He walked out with the mug in hand.

The corridor was deserted. I could hear his footsteps as he returned.

One of my hands lay on the white bedsheet as I drank the water with the other. I traced circles on the bedsheet with a trembling finger, back and forth, back and forth.

"Lie back down; you're exhausted."

Even after I lay back down, I kept stroking the bedsheet—an embroidered sheet so white and shiny it nearly dazzled my eyes. *Not bad,* I thought. We'd never had a real bedsheet of our own. He must have read my thoughts.

"I thought we'd have to sleep on bare boards," he said. "But now we even have pillows."

He fluffed up the pillow under my head.

"Knock-knock." Someone was at the door. A large Russian female hotel attendant walked into our room followed by a Chinese attendant.

"You'll be renting the bedding too?"

"Yes."

"Fifty cents a day."

"No deal!" "No deal!"

Langhua and I both said the same thing.

The woman gathered up all the bedding: the soft pillows, the bedsheet, even the tablecloth. She tucked it all under her arm, starting with the bedsheet, and in a matter of seconds the whiteness of the room had disappeared out the door, punctuated by splashes of color in the woman's babushka.

4

I got up—rubbery legs, growling stomach, and all—opened our wicker trunk, and removed the bedroll.

The room looked as though it had been pillaged. The bed was covered with a puffy straw mat, the dilapidated wooden table was scarred with black smudges and white circles, even the large rattan chair seemed to have undergone a change in color.

We passed the time before dinner hugging and kissing on the straw mat.

We laid dinner out on the table—black khleb* and salt.

Things really started happening after dinner.

Three or four policemen dressed in black, rifles slung over their shoulders or wearing bayonets at their belts, entered the room. Right away they pinned Langhua's arms behind his back. (He had stripped to the waist to wash up, so his arms were still wet.) The men then opened our trunk and searched its contents.

"We received a report from the hotel that you have a gun. Is that true?" asked a man with a bayonet at his belt. The man then looked under the bed and brought out a sword rolled up in paper. After unrolling the paper, he exposed the sword and shook the tassel.

"Where'd you get this?"

The Russian hotel manager, who had been standing in the doorway, gave an embarrassed wave of the hand and blushed a bright red.

The police wanted to take Langhua to the station house, and he was prepared to go with them. But he wasn't going to go quietly.

"How come you have to carry out your searches like this? Why all the abuse?"

The police finally softened a bit and released their grip on him. He had forgotten that he was naked from the waist up—his arms were dry by then.

*The Russian generic term for bread.

5

The incident had stemmed from earlier that day when the White Russian had come to collect the rent. The room let for two yuan a day, sixty yuan a month. We had only five yuan between us, minus the fifty cents we had paid the carter to bring us over with our things.

"Your rent—give me!" the White Russian had said. He must have known that we were broke. He agitated, seemingly afraid that we'd try to skip out on the rent. Once he had two one-yuan bills safely in hand, he had said: "One month sixty yuan. Give it tomorrow!" The rent had originally been thirty yuan a month, but he had doubled it as soon as the Sungari River threatened to overflow its banks. Gesturing with his hand, he had stared at us coldly. "You tomorrow move out. You tomorrow go!"

"We're not leaving," Langhua had said. "We're staying."

"You have to go. I'm the manager . . ."

Langhua had reached under the bed and taken out his sword, brandishing it under the White Russian's nose.

"You get the hell out of here! If you don't, I'll have your head!"

The man had fled in panic and had run to the station house, reporting that we had a dangerous weapon. Since it had remained rolled up in paper, he had assumed the weapon to be a gun, never suspecting that it was a sword.

The police confiscated the sword and left, but not before giving us a warning: "If the Japanese MPs had found this, things would have really gone badly for you. They'd have said you belonged to a terrorist group. You'd have been in hot water for sure then. We'll hold on to this overnight, and you can claim it at the station house tomorrow."

After the police left, we put out the lamp and locked the door. Light from the street lamps shone in through the window—a cold, subdued light. We fell asleep. As we slept, our thoughts kept returning to the Chinese policemen—how superior they were to the Japanese MPs.

Dawn broke on our second day, the second day since we had been kicked out of the home of a friend.

2

A Snowy Day

I HAD slept round the clock. Now I was wide awake. Darkness slowly engulfed our little room. I had awakened with a sore back, sore shoulders, and a growing hunger. I got out of bed, lit the lamp, and sat back down on the edge of the bed for a while; then I moved over to the rattan chair, where I straightened my hair and rubbed my sleepy eyes. I was feeling melancholic and sort of empty, almost as though I had been transported to the depths of a coal mine, all alone and without even a lantern to light my way down. Small though the room was, I had the sensation of being in the middle of a vast deserted public square. The walls enclosing me seemed farther away than the heavens themselves; I was all alone, completely cut off from the outside world. It all boiled down to this: I had an empty stomach.

Street noises streamed in through the window, but the corridor outside our third-floor room was deathly still. My attention was riveted to the sound of footsteps every time someone passed down the corridor. Leather-soled shoes resounded past my door, followed by even louder taps from the high-heeled shoes of a woman in a hurry. Occasionally, groups of people—men and women—clattered down the corridor past my door. My ears pricked up at every sound that came from the corridor, but I didn't need to open the door; I knew without looking that Langhua still hadn't returned.

The window was high up on the wall, like in a prison cell. I raised my head to look out the window at the swirling snowflakes falling outside the building. Some of them stuck to the windowpane, melting on the glass and forming rivulets of water, turning the window into a mass of meandering, aimless streaks.

Why did snowflakes dance in the air? How meaningless it all seemed. It dawned on me that I was just like those snowflakes, leading a meaningless existence. I was sitting in the chair, empty-handed, doing nothing; my mouth was open but there was nothing to eat. I was exactly like a completely idled machine.

A noise in the corridor startled me. *If I'm not mistaken, that'll be Langhua!* The muffled footsteps of someone wearing cloth-soled shoes drew up to my door. I nearly leapt to my feet. I was so worried—*poor Langhua! He's probably freezing out there. I'll bet he hasn't brought any bread back with him.*I opened the door, and was face to face with the hotel attendant.

"You want dinner?"

"How much is it?"

"Sixty cents a meal or fifteen yuan a month."

I shook my head without a moment's hesitation. I was afraid he might bring the food inside, make me eat it, then force me to pay for it. After he walked off, I gravely closed the door. That simple action cut me off completely from the laughter of other rooms, from the aromas of other people's food. I was isolated from the rest of the world by a single closed door.

Only the sound of Langhua's crepe-soled shoes scraping along the doorsill brought my fantasies to an end— the tray in the attendant's hands, meat cakes, roasted sweet potatoes, thick slices of spongy bread . . .

Langhua's thin jacket was drenched, his pant legs

were all wet and muddy, and the soles of his shoes were so full of holes that his socks were soaked.

He lay down on the bed to get warm, covering everything but his feet with the quilt. I wiped the frozen mud splotches off his feet with some rags.

"Hungry?" he asked me, as he lay there stiffly, sort of like a simpleton.

I was nearly in tears. "No," I said, keeping my head so low that my face nearly touched the soles of his frozen feet.

His clothing was soaked through, so I went out and bought some steamed buns. We sat at the table, which was bare of everything but our steaming toothbrush mug. The mug kept us company as we ate the steamed buns. When they were gone, we looked hungrily at the few remaining copper coins.

"Had enough?" he asked me.

"Yes," I said. "How about you?"

"Me, too."

Someone began playing a concertina in the next room. Was it a tune dedicated to the misery of life? It was such a mournful tune!

I opened the little window by standing on the table. That little window was our sole link with the outside world. Through it we maintained contact with the skyline—roofs and chimneys—the falling snow, the dark, floating, moisture-laden clouds—street lamps, policemen, hawkers, beggars . . . The streets were noisy and bustling.

We could no longer hear the concertina in the next room.

3

He Goes Job Hunting

He was a freezing, starving dog!

There, at the head of the stairs, at the farthest end of the corridor, his wet cap disappearing around the corner, his shoes trailing wet, muddy tracks on the highly polished floorboards.

It was still early in the morning, before the sun had begun sending its rays down the length of the corridor. But already many of the doors were adorned with rings of khleb. The milkman had very gently placed steaming bottles of snow-white milk in front of the doorways. It was *so* tempting. I could almost smell the khleb—I could almost believe that one of those fat rings had been placed right under my nose. I was growing desperate after too many days of having too little to eat. My capacity for food had already shrunk considerably. With no money to buy anything, I was being tyrannized by those unattainable rings of khleb.

The hotel began to stir as guests stepped out into the corridor and called for the attendants; doors opened, doors closed, wash basins were filled with water. Foreign women wasted no time, starting their day with their loud talk and high-pitched laughs. But my little room was so poorly lighted that even the flying specks of dust were invisible; it was so quiet that the table was about to fall asleep in the corner of the room, along with the rattan chair; it was so quiet that the ceiling seemed as high as the heavens themselves. Everything was utterly distant from me, as though it were repulsed by my very existence.

Langhua still hadn't returned by afternoon. I stood in the doorway several times and watched some of the foreign women walk downstairs in their red skirts and blue skirts—proud smiles adorning their lipsticked mouths, their high-heeled shoes making crisp tapping sounds on the steps. Dark-faced and bony-figured gypsy women with long dangling earrings were escorted upstairs by moon-faced and bearded men—these odd-looking couples were preceded by attendants who ushered them into their rooms. Some time later, a group of foreign children walked noisily upstairs, munching on melon seeds and leaving water tracks on the floor of the corridor from the ice on their shoes.

Langhua still hadn't returned, even after I'd had my fill of watching these comings and goings. I began prowling up and down the corridor, passing furtively by the other rooms until the guests inside must have assumed that I was either a thief or a beggar. But I didn't realize that at the time. I just kept prowling the hall with a wan face and a faded, oversized blue shirt.

The sudden arrival of two young foreign women of identical height at the head of the stairs took me by surprise.

"Aiya!" One of them pointed to me and said, "You—very pretty!"

The other woman stepped back as though she were shying away from me. The two of them swished the fronts of their skirts to show them off for me.

"You—very pretty!"

I ignored them. I figured it must have started snowing outside again, since water was dripping from their caps.

I ran back to my room and looked out the window to see if I was right about the snow. Langhua had gone out in the same wet clothes he had been wearing the night before. The moment I threw the window open, it closed by itself from the weight of the accumulated snow.

Langhua was back, water dripping steadily from the brim of his cap.

11

"It must be freezing out there!" I said as I took his cap from him.

He raised his leg to show me his trouser cuff. His pant leg was cold and stiff to the touch. He took my hand in his and said, "Child, you must be starving!"

"Not really," I said. How could I tell him I was hungry? His clothing was frozen stiff from his search for something to eat.

He waited a while longer before taking out twenty yuan and showing it to me. I was dumbstruck. Where had he gotten that?

4

The Tutor

TWENTY yuan. For that sum he had become a tutor.

Today was to be his first day on the job. He awoke at the crack of dawn, seemingly in higher spirits than usual. I hurried into the corridor to pour some water, happy to be doing my part. My heart was bursting with joy, and as I made the bed, I sang snatches from one song after another. Then I sat on the edge of the bed and dangled my legs happily, the hem of my blouse dancing way down around my shins. I dashed out into the corridor several times to look for the man who made deliveries from his basket of bread. *He should eat some sort of snack,* I thought. *He has to begin teaching at eight o'clock. With the weather so cold and his clothing so thin, he should at least have something in his stomach.*

But there was no trace in the corridor of the man with his heaping basketful of bread.

Langhua probably agreed that he should eat something now that he had a job as a tutor, for after I found the man downstairs, Langhua bought some food from him when his big, rectangular basket appeared at our doorway. Langhua was like a greedy house lizard, intent on satisfying his appetite by snatching pieces of bread, round pastries, and black khleb rings out of the basket. Looking at those muscular arms of his, I sensed that nothing would satisfy him short of taking the whole basket into the room. Finally, though, he paid for what he had taken, resolutely handing back the basket and hurrying into the room to eat his food.

He left before eight o'clock and was back shortly after nine. He went out again just before dusk. He returned an hour later, in a state of excitement, as though his life had suddenly taken on meaning. This time he had brought a small bundle home with him; in it, he said, were two articles of clothing that he had pawned some time ago and had today retrieved from the pawnshop. With obvious enthusiasm, he pulled out a lined full-length gown and a small sweater.

"You wear the lined gown and I'll wear the sweater," he instructed me.

The two of us put on the garments without a moment's hesitation. The sweater fit him perfectly. The lined gown was a different matter. After I put it on, not only could I not see my feet but both of my hands were swallowed up by the sleeves. The wide sleeves of the gown were so big I had the sudden feeling that a huge sack was hanging from my shoulders, but that alone was enough to make me feel that it fit just right. I couldn't have been happier with it.

Electric lights illuminated an entire city's populace. I had money in my pocket, so the two of us walked down the street with complete assuredness. We crossed over the streetcar tracks and passed through the ghetto street with all its hustle and bustle.

Langhua opened a glass door that had seen better

days—sheets of paper were plastered over its broken panes. He turned to me and said, "This is a nice little café. All the ricksha pullers and workers eat here."

I followed him in. The entire café had only three large tables, which seemed unusual to me. The customers were clustered shoulder to shoulder, seated around the tables. The café was so packed, there was barely room to turn around, and I wondered where I was going to sit. There wasn't an empty spot at any of the three tables. Sticking my hand out of my sleeve, I tugged at Langhua's arm and said, "There isn't a vacant table, so where will we sit?"

"People don't worry about etiquette when they eat here," he said. "Just find a seat anywhere you can." Langhua, who was much more at home than I, hung his hat on a peg on the wall. A waiter walked over and wiped off the table with a greasy towel, saying to one of the diners as he did so, "Move over, please. Make a little room."

Langhua wedged himself in on the bench when the man moved over. As for me, I perched on the owner's stool, which the waiter had moved to the head of the table. It didn't seem to matter if we existed or not. Before long, several small plates of food were placed in front of us on the table. I spotted some steamed meat on a little round chopping board. Langhua dashed over and said, "Slice a nickel's worth of pig's head for us!"

The man there took up his knife, wiped it off on the filthy apron he was wearing, then began slicing some of the meat with exceptional skill and show. *How did Langhua know it was pig's head?* I wondered. But in no time at all, I was dining on pig's head. After that, I noticed a big firepot in which some food was simmering. I really wanted to know what was being cooked, but I didn't have the nerve to ask and was too embarrassed to get up and just walk around inside the café.

"Go take a look."

"There's nothing good in there," Langhua said as he walked over for a look. But the opposite was true: the grease-covered pot was filled with meat dumplings.

"How about having some of those?" the proprietor quickly urged.

We didn't answer right away, and he prompted our silence by adding, "They're delicious."

But it was the cost, not the taste that had given us pause (meat dishes were sure to be more expensive). With five or six plates of food already in front of us, we figured that was enough. The man looked at me. I looked back at him.

"With all this food, we'd better pass on the meat dumplings," I said.

"They come in a nice broth." He had said the magic word, and I decided that I'd like some after all. The moment my decision was made, a plate of meat dumplings appeared on the table in front of us.

People were coming and going through the dilapidated glass door: some were wearing tattered leather caps and fur-lined gowns, and some were in paint-spattered work clothes—bearded old house painters and young teenagers with shrill voices.

The floor was just damp enough to make me uncomfortable. But the door kept opening and closing; people kept entering and leaving. An old woman with a young child in her arms stood just outside the door begging. Whenever someone opened the door, she pleaded: "Have pity! Please have pity! Give the child something to eat!" But she never pushed the door open herself. Eventually the wait must have been too much for her, for she followed a customer into the café. She stopped just inside the door, not daring to close it herself, making it clear that as soon as someone gave her something to eat, she'd leave. The atmosphere inside the café suddenly grew cold. Langhua was just about to give her a steamed bun when the proprietor held out his hand and said, "There's too many of 'em; don't give her any!"

One of the diners next to the door slammed it shut, forcing the woman outside. "Damn!" he muttered. "It's cold as hell in here. Who in his right mind would leave the door open!"

Someone else in the crowd voiced his opinion. "If that'd been a young lady instead of an old woman, you'd have thrown your arms around her instead of pushing her out the door, or at least you'd have given her the once over."

Just about everyone inside the café laughed, but I wasn't used to hearing talk like that. It angered me.

Langhua bought a small pot of wine to go with the pig's head, and I helped him drink it. One of the other diners at our table was eating only some pickled vegetables and thin gruel. When his check came it was for less than ten cents. Then ours came: each of the small dishes of food had cost two cents, and we had ordered five. Also, we had ordered five cents' worth of pig's head, five cents' worth of wine, and eight cents' worth of meat dumplings, not to mention the eight big steamed buns.

We weren't prepared for what hit us as we walked out of the café: the air was freezing cold, and stars filled the sky with their brightness. We hurried over toward the street where streetcars passed us with bells clanging.

"Did you have enough to eat?" he asked.

"I sure did."

As we walked by a small food stand, I stopped and bought a couple of pieces of hard candy, one for him and one for me. We sucked on the candy as we climbed the stairs.

"You really do look like a big sack," he remarked to me after he had finished his candy.

I looked over and sized him up, and he didn't look so presentable himself. We both stopped in front of the

16

downstairs mirror and admired our reflections. He was wearing his cap down low on his forehead. The back of his head looked all but forgotten, bulging out a long, long way beyond the brim of his cap. Who ever heard of putting a small, nearly brimless cap on such a big head! That little cap of his couldn't have been more inappropriate, resting there on the top of his head, forever on the verge of falling off. It looked like a crow perched on a rooftop, ready to take wing at any moment. And the student uniform someone had given him, which was both too short and too big for him, was beyond description.

We entered the room like a couple of kids, sticking our tongues out at each other. His piece of candy had been red, so he stuck out a bright red tongue; my tongue was green. Following this little display, a worried look came over his face, and he began to tap the tabletop with his fingernails.

"Have you ever seen anything less thrilling than me as a tutor? All I do is come and go like a little beggar in the freezing cold!"

As he talked, still tapping the table, I noticed that the sleeve above his hand was all tattered and marked with loose threads. His threadbare clothes didn't bother me as much as the cold he had to endure.

Neither of us said a word for a long time. The light from the lamp shone steadily on our faces. I told him I'd mend the sleeve of his shirt after I bought a needle and some thread the next day. My remark caused him to look down at his sleeve, and his face glazed suddenly, as though he were lost in a dream. His lips parted slightly and somewhat unnaturally, although he didn't say a word.

After we turned off the lamp, the room was illuminated by the moonlight streaming in through the window. We huddled under a single quilt and pillowed our heads with some dog-eared books. In the adjoining

17

room, the concertina continued to play its plaintive song of the joys and sorrows of life on earth. The music was companion to Langhua's words as his heart slowly emerged from its imprisonment:

"Minzi—Miss Minzi mended this for me. But that's all in the past, and the past holds no meaning. I've told you before—I was a crazy man then. It wasn't really over until that last letter. What I mean by "over" is that she sent no more letters, ever. The letter was so unexpected that I didn't know whether to believe it or not. I was in a state of shock for days afterward—before that, she often wrote that she loved me, that she'd love me no matter what. But in that last letter she really gave me hell. I still find it hard to believe, but that's the way it goes."

He walked over and picked up the sweater to show me. "You see these peach-colored threads—she mended this for me—Minzi mended it."

He put the light out again, and still the concertina sang from the adjoining room. As he talked, he spoke her name—"Minzi, Minzi"—the sound as soft as running water.

"She was beautiful, with her dark black eyebrows—her lips were so—so red!" Just then he squeezed my hand tightly under the quilt. *I'm not her*, I thought to myself.

"Her lips were a bright, bright red—ah—" he said again.

The clattering of horsehooves resounded loudly on the cobblestones outside. All the neighboring courtyards must be in a deep sleep, I imagined.

5

Visitors

A KNOCK at the door. A heavy-set man in a silk Mandarin gown walked in. He said he had come to study, which took me by surprise. He was forty or fifty years old and a merchant, besides. What could he want to study? Finally, after a long time, he said he wanted to study the works of the philosopher Zhuangzi. He said he felt no need to study any modern works, since they were too easy to understand and didn't count as "learning."

What was Langhua going to do? "Sure," he said. "I can teach you."

The heavy-set man said he also wanted to write one essay per week for his teacher to correct. Langhua said that was fine with him. As far as he was concerned, anything that brought in some money—tuition money—was fine with him.

On yet another morning, a young man came to our door. Langhua wasn't home, so the young man sat and waited on the straw mat covering our bed. He appeared to have consumption. As he sat looking at some old newspapers that were spread out on the bed, he asked me, "The notice posted outside your door says martial arts lessons are five yuan a month. Do you think he'll take less?"

"We can talk about that later."

He sat there very properly, appearing quite listless. Ten more minutes passed like that! Why hadn't Langhua returned? I was starting to worry. Earning a little tuition money was like a business deal, and this was one business deal I didn't think we'd be able to pull off, since the young man kept saying he was going to leave.

"Wait just a little while longer. He'll be right back. I'm sure he will."

But he couldn't wait. As he was on his way out, he said, "I've got consumption. I work at the Taloshin, a department store. I've been there a year, but my illness hasn't gotten any better. The doctor told me to get some exercise. Medicine is so expensive I can't afford it. I figured that a little exercise was better than nothing at all. I didn't know someone here taught martial arts till I read an ad in yesterday's paper. When the teacher comes home, would you ask him if he'd lower the tuition a little?"

So after placing an ad in the paper for work as a tutor, we had people coming to seek cures for their diseases, to study the writings of Zhuangzi, and even to master the art of leaping onto roofs and vaulting over walls like mythical swordsmen. Did the master know how to leap onto roofs and vault over walls? they asked.

Langhua was out one day when another man came, but this person left without even taking a seat. As soon as he entered the room, he spotted the grass mat on the bed and the rolled-up quilt at the head of the bed, losing gray stuffing out of several holes. I wanted to fold it properly, but it was too late. The man took a long look at the pair of tattered shoes on the floor. Glints of light reflected off his cane and his eyeglasses. As far as he was concerned, the martial-arts master was nothing more than a beggar.

6

The Basket Carrier

THE man with the basket, that big basket of his, oval loaves of bread, round bread—the tempting aroma of wheat was there with him, waiting for me in the corridor every morning.

I counted it out—three, five, ten—I handed him all the copper coins I had. A loaf of black bread now lay on the table. The first thing Langhua did when he got home was scoop a hole out of the bread; before he had even taken off his cap he was busy chewing a piece of bread. Then he started looking for some salt. The cold air he had brought in with him gave off a rank odor. Drops of water dripped off his nose every once in a while as he ate the bread.

"Come and have some!"

"I'll be right there." I took the toothbrush mug downstairs to get some water. When I got back, about the only thing left of the bread was the hard outer crust.

He quickly said, "I really ate fast. How could I have eaten so fast? Boy, am I selfish. Men sure are selfish." I handed him the mug filled with water. He wasn't going to eat any more. I told him to go ahead, but he refused. "I've had enough," he said. "I'm full. I've already eaten your half; isn't that enough? Men are no good; they're only interested in themselves. Since you've just gotten well you should get enough to eat."

He chatted on about wanting to open a "school" where he could teach martial arts and also teach a little of this and that. As he told me all this he was reaching for the crust. Then his other hand moved into action and, before he knew it, he had twisted off another piece, put it into his mouth, and swallowed it. He reached out again, but this time he said, "I shouldn't eat any more. I've had enough already."

His cap was still on his head, so I reached over and took it off for him, putting another piece of breadcrust into his mouth at the same time.

When he drank the water, it was the same thing all over—he didn't hand any to me until I asked him.

"I'll take you out to a restaurant for dinner tonight." That came as a surprise: how could we eat in a restaurant if we had no money?

"We'll just get up and leave after we've eaten. In times like this, we have to eat or we'll starve to death." He went out to get some more water.

On the following day, the bread-filled basket was waiting for me out in the corridor. But this time I didn't open the door. Other people were out there buying bread from him. Even with the door closed I thought I could still smell the fragrance of wheat. I began to be frightened by the bread. It wasn't that I wanted to eat any. I was afraid that the bread would swallow me up.

"Khleb, khleb!" In Harbin we called bread "khleb." The breadseller was rapping on our door and calling out to me. With fear in my heart, I made my selection and said to him, "I'll pay you tomorrow. I don't have any change right now."

Even tutors rested on Sunday. But resting was all he could do. We had nothing to eat for breakfast. The man with the basket was knocking on our door. Langhua jumped down off the bed with the agility of a cat, briskly and noiselessly. I didn't move a muscle. The khleb was right there in our doorway. Langhua was barefoot, wearing only a pair of shorts, with his shirt draped over his shoulders and his chest completely exposed.

A loaf of black bread cost ten cents. I also wanted five cents' worth of khleb, which the man started to string together.

"No need for that," I said. I was going to eat it right away. I propped myself up in bed and raised my head, looking for all the world like a silkworm that has just seen some mulberry leaves.

But it wasn't to be: right before my very eyes, the man wrenched the bread out of Langhua's hands and did the same with the five khleb rings.

"Can't we pay you for everything tomorrow?"

"No. And I want the five cents you owe me from yesterday right now!"

I licked my lips with my wet tongue; not only must we go without any khleb, but every last copper we had went away with the man.

"What will we eat for breakfast?"

"Got any ideas?" He locked the door and came to bed, where he plastered his icy body up against mine.

7

Hunger

RINGS of khleb hung from other people's doors up and down the corridor. Dawn seemed not yet to have arrived, but the lights already were turned off. The corridor was still suffused with the drowsy appearance left behind by the night. A hotel attendant mopped the floor, panting as he worked. I hadn't intended to wake up so early, but I was awake, nonetheless, and I couldn't fall back to sleep.

The light in the corridor bathroom was still on, giving off the same pale glow as at night. Dawn hadn't broken, but rings of khleb already hung from other people's doors. Bottles of milk also stood neatly in front of other people's rooms. They had only to wake up to have something to eat and drink; naturally, that luxury was reserved for others—it was their affair and had nothing to do with me.

I turned on the lamp. Langhua was in bed, sleeping so soundly that his even breathing passed through the air without making a ripple. Not a person was stirring in the corridor. All three floors of the hotel were bathed in sleep. The quiet grew increasingly enticing, urging a growing determination. Still not a sound in the corridor. The quieter it seemed, the stronger the enticement grew. My plan was taking hold of me: *Go take it. Now's the time. So what if it's stealing! Do it anyway!*

Stealthily, I turned the key in the lock, not making a sound. I poked my head out to take a look. Some khleb hung on the door directly opposite and on the doors on either side. *It's almost light outside!* The milky whiteness of the bottles nearly dazzled me. The khleb seemed larger than usual. But I took nothing—nothing. My heart was on fire, my ears were burning. *Stealing!* Words from my childhood flashed back into my mind: *A child who steals pears is most shameful of all.* I stood there for the longest time flattened up against the now-closed door. I must have looked like a soulless paper doll stuck to the door. I guess that's what I must have looked like. The sounds of passing vehicles out on the street brought me back to my senses: the clatter of horses' hooves, the crunching sound of tires. I hugged myself tightly; my head drooped onto my chest. *I'm hungry!* I said to myself. *I'm not stealing!*

I opened the door a second time. This time I was determined. *So what if it's stealing!* I'd steal, even if it were only a few khleb rings. This was for my hunger, for *his* hunger.

For the second time I failed, and there was no need to try for a third. I knew what I had to do: I climbed back into bed, turned off the lamp, and nudged Langhua sharply a couple of times. This didn't wake him up, and I guess I was really afraid that it might. In that moment, when I was "stealing," Langhua was my enemy; had I had a mother, she, too, would have been my enemy.

Dawn had broken! The people stirred and awoke; so did the streets.

The tutor had no money to buy anything to eat, but he had to hold class anyway, and he had to practice his martial arts. He drank a cup of hot water and left. The khleb outside in the corridor had long since disappeared; it had been eaten.

24

It was noon. And I had had nothing to eat since the night before. My limbs had grown weak; my belly was like a ball with the air kicked out of it.

The window was high in the center of the wall, like a skylight. I ascended up, up through the window, utterly naked, rising up on the rays of the sun. The streets below my feet were laid out in straight lines; the buildings alongside were varied and angular. The factory chimneys, looking like so many gigantic posts, dotted the crisscrossed streets below. Trees with nothing but bare branches. Clouds in the sky forming a myriad of shapes. My hair was blown every which way by the winds in the sky; my shirttail fluttered in the wind.*
The city streets and a map of many colors thrown randomly together hung in front of my eyes. A thin layer of frost covered rooftops and naked branches. The entire city was a layer of silver, off of which the sun's rays danced and glittered. I could hear my shirttail fluttering in the winds. I was cold. I was like a person standing all alone and lonely on a mountain peak. For a fleeting moment, the frost of the rooftops turned from silver into a layer of snowflakes, or ice, or some other even colder and more forbidding substance engulfing me. I began to merge with the ice.

I wrapped the quilt around my shoulders and stood up to look out the window, exposing only my head and upper torso, not my whole body. A woman stood in the door of a pharmacy begging for some coins. She was holding one child by the hand and cradling an even smaller one, in the front part of her coat. None of the people coming out of the pharmacy paid any attention to her, nor did any of the passersby. They apparently felt that she had no right to have children—that the poor had no right—and if she had children anyway, starving was what they deserved.

*The narrator has apparently forgotten that she is naked.

From where I stood I could see only half of the street. The woman had apparently walked over underneath my window, since the sound of her child's crying grew nearer.

"Master, Mistress, take pity, take pity." I couldn't see who she was following, but I could hear her every sound clearly, even though she was three stories below. I was sure that she was stumbling along as fast as she could, gasping her pleas, "Master—Master—please take pity!"

She was exactly like me: I was sure she had gone without breakfast and maybe last night's dinner as well. I was affected by the sound of her voice as she moved anxiously back and forth beneath my window. My stomach began to rumble, and my intestines protested without pause.

Langhua still hadn't returned, so with what was I going to fill my belly? The table? The straw mat?

Walkways bathed in sunlight, pedestrians, hawkers, beggars—just watching them was exhausting! I yawned and climbed down from the window.

The window frosted up as soon as I closed it. Before long, tears were streaming down the pane of glass! At first, only a few streaks, but then the tears ran in a torrent down the glass! The face of the window was covered in tears, just like the face of the beggar-woman on the street below.

I sat in that little room, feeling like a hungry caged chicken. I just wanted to close my eyes and rest, to stay quiet for a while without really falling asleep.

"Knock-knock." *Who could that be?* I ran over to the door to open it. There stood my art teacher from the school I had attended three years earlier.

He still liked to tell jokes as much as he had then; in fact, the only changes I could detect were that he had put on a little weight and that his eyes seemed a little smaller. He talked on and on about nothing in particular. His daughter, a young girl dressed in a red cheongsam with a floral print, over which she wore a black velvet jacket, sat very prettily in our rattan chair; she was growing impatient.

"Let's go now, Papa." How could a young girl know anything about life? Girls such as she only understood a pretty appearance; how could they know anything about life?

"Do you live here alone?" Mr. Cao asked me.

"Yes." I don't know why I said that, since I was obviously living with Langhua. Why would I tell him that I lived alone?

It was almost as though these few years of being apart had never happened, as though I were still a student in the school where he taught.

"It's better to be by yourself. That way you can devote all your time and energy to your art. Since you now prefer literature over painting, you should devote yourself totally to literature. The only full heart is the one loyally devoted to art. Beauty can be found only in art. It's the only true beauty. 'Love' is harder to figure out. If love is based on sex, then it's better to satisfy your sexual desires whenever they arise by taking whomever comes along, as long as it's someone of the opposite sex. Love is love. Real 'love' is hard to come by, so a person's better off loving art. You'll have a better chance of keeping your heart filled."

"Papa, let's go!" How could a young girl know anything about life. She only understood a pretty appearance. She looked around the room, finding nothing of interest. The bed was covered with nothing but a straw mat.

"Okay, we're going," Mr. Cao said as he looked at his daughter. "Look at me. Married at thirteen. Isn't that right? Cao Yun's already fifteen!"

"Papa, let's go. Okay?"

He was still talking about his marriage at thirteen.

Nearly all the students at school knew that Mr. Cao had been married at the age of thirteen.

"Papa, let's go. Okay?"

He dropped a bank note on the table and left. I had written to him asking for that.

Langhua still hadn't come home. My first thoughts should have been of my hunger, but I was so enchanted by reminiscences of my youthful student days that hunger was the furthest thing from my mind. I knew only that youth is the most important time in a person's life. I wasn't old yet, but I couldn't shake the feeling that my youth was gone! Gone!

I was deep in thought for a long time. The pulsing of my heart swelled from moment to moment, like waves in the ocean.

Be practical! Only selfish people balk at giving up their youth. Hunger and cold is all there is: there is no youth.

The little café we had stayed away from for so many days—now we were back there, eating and drinking. "You must be tired. Aren't your legs sore? You must have had to walk fifteen li, including Inner City and Outer City," I remarked to him.

As long as there was food to eat, he was satisfied, and so was I. Everything else was forgotten!

By now this café was one of my old haunts, so instead of waiting for him to sit, I pulled out the first available chair and sat right down. I knew the menu by heart—spicy bok choy, mustard bean curd . . . braised fish in soy sauce. Now how could they call it braised *fish* in soy sauce? Where was the fish? They just cooked fish bones in some soy sauce to give it a little flavor, and that was their "braised fish." I was confident that I could order a meal without adding up all the prices and still not go over ten cents, so I called out our order in a loud voice. I wasn't afraid; spending money was nothing to be afraid of.

After we returned home we talked for a while and drank some water before turning in.

"Well, we didn't starve this time! And we've got enough left over for several more days."

We put out the lamp and slept the night through, feeling very content and very secure.

8

The New Apartment

WE were moving! And what does "moving" mean? It means changing one nest for another.

A single horse-drawn cart carried two people and a willow trunk, which held all their belongings. The cart traveled down the street—vehicles on the road, pedestrians on the walkways, mannequins inside display windows.

Motorcars passed by. A horse pulling someone else's cart trotted past us. A pair of young lovers were seated in this other cart. Curls peeked out from under the young woman's hat and danced in the air; the man's long arms seemed to serve no purpose and were just there for show behind the woman's back. The cart passed us—a pair of lovers out for a spin, no doubt about it. For us, it was only moving day. Clouds like pools of water or ice melting in the spring floated in the sky. I raised my head to watch them. As the wind blew past my ears, it whistled.

Here we are: 25 Market Street.*

He was carrying the trunk under his arm; I was carrying the wash basin. We passed through a long court-

*The original does not give the number.

29

yard, all the way to the last building at the rear. Langhua opened the door.

"Go on in," he said.

We had now moved our home; this was to be our new "home."

A little boy wearing a pair of huge boots came running and hopping over, shouting at the top of his lungs, "Ma! My teacher's here, my teacher's here!"

So this was his martial-arts disciple.

The steel-framed bed we had borrowed wouldn't fit through the door. And it wouldn't fit through the window, either. Were we really going to have to sleep on the floor? Just lie there naked? What would we use for bedding?

"Hit it with an axe, Master." The child in the high boots ran off to find an axe.

The steel-framed bed was standing on end, stuck in the doorway. Just as we were trying to remove the bed from the doorway, and had found that we couldn't, Langhua set to work with the axe. The air reverberated with the sound of metal banging on metal, and two shards of glass from the window over the door fell to the ground. We managed to move the bed inside, where we placed it in all its nakedness in the middle of the floor. We borrowed a table and two chairs from the landlord.

Langhua left, saying he was going out to buy a bucket, a cleaver, some ricebowls.

My stomach began to ache, possibly because of the cold and possibly because I was exhausted. I walked into the kitchen to take a look around. No fire burned in the stove, but a piece of kindling still smoldered inside, indicating that someone had had a fire going before we moved in.

The bedframe looked like a skeleton. Ice began to form on the window—at noontime the sun's rays were beginning to lose their warmth. Swirling winds began to pelt the window with sand and mud. I mopped the floor and cleaned the window frame with cold water. When I had finished, with nothing more to be done, my hands began to ache, then my feet.

It wasn't as quiet here as in the hotel: dogs were barking, roosters were crowing—people were clamoring and shouting.

I tried to warm my hands by placing them on the boards around the top of the stove, but that didn't work. The last ember in the stove had died out. My stomach was still aching, and I wanted to lie down on the bed. But what a bed! How could I even think of touching that icy steel?

I was hungry, I was cold, my stomach ached, and Langhua still hadn't returned; I was growing very impatient!

We didn't have a wristwatch, so I didn't even know the time. What a boring, lonely home! Like a duck that had fallen down a well, I was forlorn and completely isolated. Only my aching stomach, hunger, and cold kept me company—this was a home? This was a public square at night, totally devoid of light *and* warmth.

A loud noise came from the doorway—Langhua was back. He took the lid off the bucket so that I could look inside: it held a little cleaver, some chopsticks, bowls, a water pitcher. He took it all out, including a packet of rice wrapped in paper.

As long as he was next to me, I could put up with my hunger, and my stomachache bothered me less. He had left a straw mat outside the door, which I hadn't noticed right away.

"Did you buy that, too?" I asked him.

"I don't know how I'd get one if I *didn't* buy it."

"How much money do we have left over?"

"Left over? I'm not sure we have enough."

I started a fire in the stove after he had gone out and bought some kindling. Standing there alongside the

31

stove, I suddenly found myself preparing a meal, just like a little housewife. I burned the rape seed, and we ate the rice before it was completely cooked—it was too tough to be called gruel and too sticky to be called steamed rice. So I was a housewife. How else could I have cooked a real meal? Who but a housewife would know how to cook a meal?

That night the landlord came over, evidently to pay a courtesy call on his son's teacher, for our landlord was the father of the child in the boots.

"Third Elder Sister's here!" the boy called out a few moments later, after knocking on the door.

I wouldn't have recognized her anywhere, but she told me that she had seen me almost every day at school, either on the athletic field or in the assembly hall. She even remembered my name.

"It's only been three years. I don't know how I could have forgotten so completely—which class were you in?" I asked her.

"The ninth."

"The ninth. You mean Guo Xiaoxian's class? Guo Xiaoxian used to play ball every day, and I still remember her."

"Right! I played basketball, too."

But I simply didn't remember her at all. The person sitting across from me was a total stranger.

"You were in your teens then, I suppose."

"Fifteen!"

"Then you were too young. Most of the kids in school didn't pay much attention to the younger students." I thought for a moment, then smiled.

She appeared to be older than I, with her perm and her lipstick. My thoughts had taken me back in time. Actually, since I was now twenty-two, compared with her I would have to be considered old. And the candlelight made things worse; in a mirror, if I'd had one, I'm sure I'd have looked older and more worn out than a woman of thirty or more.

"Third Elder Sister, your teacher's here."

"I have a Russian lesson," she said, as she stood up in response to her younger brother's shout.

She was so refreshingly cheerful and so full of girlish charm. Her tall figure, with its thin waist, glided past me as she walked out the door.

9

The Last Piece of Kindling

I LIT a fire in the stove, but it went out, so I lit it again. It went out again. By the third time, I was upset, and could no longer control my anger. I might as well freeze to death or starve. Since I couldn't get a fire going, cooking would be impossible. That same morning I had burned my hand twice on the iron gate of the stove and had even scorched one of my fingernails. Some tongues of flame had darted out through the iron gate. I had directed my anger at the flames—I still hadn't lost my little-girl airs. I looked over toward the window. My heart was sad. My feet were so cold they ached. I was about to cry, but the tears never came, even after a long time. I wasn't a pampered little girl any longer, so why cry?

When I wanted to cook our dinner, only a single piece of kindling remained. How could I possibly start a fire with that! A single piece of kindling was about one-twentieth of what I needed for such a big stove.

"Come to bed. It's freezing in here. When we get hungry we can eat some bread," Langhua said to me as he shook the quilt.

I took off my socks and tucked up my legs under the covers. I would have liked nothing more than to be able to tuck them tightly against my belly to warm them, but that was impossible. My legs were too long. What inconvenient things these legs were—useless! Even under the covers I was trembling from the cold. A thick coat of frost had accumulated on the window. The walls shone a pale green, lined in gold, which made me feel even colder. We could see our breath. The frost-covered window pane looked like a river covered with willow catkins as fine as a layer of down. We never knew when night fell or when dawn broke; inside this secluded room neither light nor darkness entered. The people living inside were like mushrooms growing at the foot of a tree, never seeing the light of day. They were about to rot away. But people are not mushrooms.

I woke up in the middle of the night. I wasn't hungry, just cold. Langhua, who was naked, jumped out of bed, lit the candle, and walked into the kitchen to get a glass of cold water.

"It's freezing. Aren't you afraid of catching cold?"

"With muscles like this, you think I'm afraid of the cold?"

That's the way he was, always showing off his strength. Before he climbed back into bed, he pounded himself on the shoulders a couple of times. I shivered when I felt his body against mine. Everyone says that lovers' bodies are hotter than fire. You couldn't have convinced me.

The next day came with still only a single piece of kindling. He said we'd borrow some.

"Borrow it from whom?"

"From the Wangs."

He scribbled a note, then he stood in the doorway and yelled for his student Wang Yuxiang.

The family cook knocked on our door, a bundle of kindling in his arms.

Within half an hour my face was a bright red—at least I assumed so, since Langhua's was. Water dripped from the window, running down the glass and onto the floorboards. We could see people walking past the window; we could even see the chickens outside as they looked for food—some with black feathers, some with red feathers, some with multi-colored feathers.

"Teacher, can we practice our martial arts now? It's nine o'clock!"

"Wait till after I've had breakfast."

We had kindling but no rice, so what were we waiting for? The longer we waited, the hungrier we grew. After the martial-arts lesson, he went out to borrow some money. By the time he had borrowed the money, bought a large, thick flatcake, and returned home, only a single piece of kindling remained. What were we to do? There'd be no dinner.

That piece of kindling—we loved it, we hated it. We hated to part with it.

10

Black Khleb and White Salt

A LAYER of frost slowly gathered on our window again. It grew harder to distinguish things outside the window, man or dog.

"We're newlyweds, aren't we?" He said this in full voice, causing little ripples on the cup of water he had brought to his lips. He put down the cup, placed a pinch of salt on a piece of black bread, stuck it into his mouth, and ate it. After he had swallowed it, he added, "We're on our honeymoon!"

"That's right," I replied.

He twisted off another piece of black bread and added a pinch of salt. He tried to act like someone from a honeymoon scene in the movies, offering me the khleb and salt first, then waiting until I took a bite before returning the bread to his own mouth. It stung his tongue—too much salt, I suppose—and he gulped down some water.

"This is no good, no good at all. This sort of honeymoon'll get us both pickled!"

Salt was quite a different matter from butter; it had no sweetness, no fragrance. I sat off to the side and laughed.

No light could enter our room. Four walls and a useless window—a cave opening that had been sealed up, cutting us off completely from the outside world. Day in and day out, that's where we lived. We ate a vegetarian diet; sometimes we didn't eat at all. We were like legendary people awaiting their transformation into immortals, cultivating themselves by enduring hardships. We weren't doing badly, either, for we were enduring our share: our faces were turning yellow, our frames were growing thin; my eyes seemed to be getting larger, his cheekbones were jutting out like pieces of wood. So we were doing our part. But we still hadn't become immortals.

"Borrow money." "Borrow money." Langhua went out every day to "borrow money." He never came back with much—thirty cents, fifty cents. Only rarely did he return with as much as a whole yuan.

For many, many days the difference between life and death was black khleb and white salt.

11

Hard Times

IT was overcast for days on end. The sun never made an appearance; the sky was forever gray. What did it look like? Just like a wash of writing ink mixed in a pot of water.

I had scrubbed the boards around the stove so clean they sparkled. The bowls, the chopsticks, and the cleaver were all laid out neatly on the shelf. The first thing I did every morning was light a fire in the stove, then mop the floor and make the bed.

When the iron plates of the stove were hot, I stood close to the stove and made breakfast. The cleaver and the spoons fairly rang. The burning firewood inside the stove popped and sizzled. Steam rose from the pot, and the fragrance of onions frying in oil filled the room—I watched the onions as they danced in the boiling oil, gradually turning yellow. With my little paring knife I peeled the skins of potatoes; the light meat looked like so many pears. They were so pretty, a sort of off-white, soft but springy. I spread a piece of newspaper out over the stove boards, and onto this I cut the potatoes in thin slices. By the time the rice was cooked, the potato slices were fried and ready. I opened the window and looked outside, where I saw some puppies playing in the courtyard.

The tutor was still holding class. The fragrance of the vegetables and the rice drew me back to the stove. I sampled the food. With the spoon I stirred the rice, then the vegetables, rather hurriedly, like someone sneaking bits of food. I paced the floor, wondering why an hour-long class still wasn't over. I went back, took the lid off the pot, and ate a couple more mouthfuls. I gazed out the window again. By the time he returned, I had nearly eaten my fill. I could always tell his arrival because I had grown accustomed to hearing him loudly clear his throat as he entered the courtyard. I hid myself behind the door and waited for him to walk in. Sometimes when I did this, I would jump out, whooping loudly, before he had even walked through the door and found me.

After we had finished eating, my time was spent washing the dishes, scrubbing the pot, cleaning off the stovetop, and tidying up the shelf. If we had owned a wristwatch, I'll bet we'd have seen that by then it was already past eleven.

Three or four hours later, it was time to make dinner. He had gone out to look for some work, leaving me at home to do the cooking. I stayed home and waited for him. I began to pace the floor around the stove. Every day it was the same: eat, sleep, worry about firewood, fret over rice.

All of this had given me a clear picture. This was no longer childhood; these were the hard times. The time for getting by had begun.

12

Snow Flurries

In the evening, just as we were eating dinner, the gateman came to tell us, "Someone outside is looking for you."

We walked out across the snow-covered ground to the metal gate. Someone I had never seen before was waiting. He said he was looking for the martial-arts teacher. He followed us back to our room, stopping just outside the doorway to look for a shoe scraper—but we'd never gone quite that far in setting up house. He looked very apologetic about dirtying our floor as he entered. Our kitchen was unlighted, and as the man passed through, he nearly lost his footing because of the ice on the soles of his shoes.

An hour passed! Our noodles grew cold in the pot, and still he didn't leave. He never did say whether he wanted to study martial arts. He just sat there, wiping his mouth with a handkerchief and rubbing his eyes. *He's about to doze off!* As I stood there stirring the noodles, which had nearly frozen into a lump, I watched him gently turn up the collar of his coat. *Now he's surely going to leave!* I thought. But no. Maybe he had turned up his fur collar to keep his ears from freezing, although that couldn't happen as long as he was inside. Maybe he was planning to sleep there on the chair, after all. Is that what our room was? A place for him to sleep?

He never did say whether he wanted to study martial arts; as he was leaving, all he said was, "I'll think it over—think it over."

A lot of people came just to "think it over," some more than once. Not one of them made up his mind on the spot. Those who had decided not to study didn't want to embarrass us by saying so, or so it seemed. Those who *did* choose to study would do so only if the tuition could be lowered a little. Their constant hope seemed to be that the martial-arts teacher would voluntarily lower his tuition.

I was very uneasy during dinner. I dished up a bowl of noodles for Langhua, then one for myself. I trimmed the wick on the candle to lower the dancing flame, which was contributing to my uneasiness.

Neither of us said a word. We both stared at the candle as we ate. Outside the snow was falling more heavily. By the time I got back to the room after dumping some dirty water outside, my hair was soaked. I carried the candle over to the doorway, where I looked out to see a sheet of snow about to blot out the entire world.

Langhua threw a coat he had just borrowed over his shoulders and went to the house across the way to teach martial arts. The empty sleeves of his coat were swallowed up in the falling snowflakes. I heard him opening their door. Lights came on in their living room.

I could see by looking out my window that the snow was falling more rapidly. I was surrounded by a lonely, somber night; I began to cough, so I closed the window. I picked up a book and tried to read, but before I had finished more than a few pages, I went over and opened the window again. *Is the snow falling more heavily now? Or more lightly?* Storms and all other celestial phenomena hold a special attraction for someone who is bored. The snow was falling even faster now, the snowflakes merging with each other as they fell.

The scraping sounds of shoe leather on the road outside the main gate came through loud and clear, while footsteps inside the courtyard grew increasingly difficult to hear. I could tell that Wang Lin had returned home. I wasn't able to see if this schoolmate of mine from years before was wearing a Chinese dress or a Western one; she stood at her door and rang the bell, which was answered by their young servant girl.

"Who is it? Who's there?"

"It's me! What's wrong with your ears? 'Who is it? Who's there?'" I could hear the impatience in her voice. Proper young ladies have a youthful arrogance about them. A little bondmaid couldn't have known about that, not at all. But for the falling snow, I'm sure I would have seen a look of ignorance on the girl's face as she pulled her head back inside the door.

I went back and read some more, then came back and watched the falling snow. I had read several pages, but about what? I had no idea. All I could think of was the heavy snowfall outside. This colder weather meant that I'd probably have to stay inside the room from now on. Langhua had neither a cap nor a fur collar on his coat, so sooner or later his ears would get frostbitten.

Inside the room, as long as a fire burned in the stove, that's where I stood; and if the weather got any colder, I could go so far as to sit on the stovetop till I was "done." Whenever we ran out of firewood, I wrapped the quilt around me and sat on the bed. My life revolved around the bed, day and night. How could I go outside? Could I walk down the street with a quilt wrapped around me? No, that would never do!

I stuck my feet straight into the stove opening as I sat on the chair and read. But I wasn't actually reading, just going through the motions. My heart wasn't in it.

As soon as Langhua walked into the room, he asked me, "You roasting a couple of hams?"

"Is it snowing heavily?" I asked in return.

"Look at my coat!" He was dusting the snow off with a face towel.

The snow made me uneasy, terrified me, brought me every imaginable kind of nightmare all night long. A litter of piglets falling into a pit of snow. Sparrows frozen to death on telephone wires—even though they're all dead, they're still perched on the wires. Stiffened human bodies in the wilderness laid out in row after row under great white trees—some of their arms or legs are missing, having snapped off from the torsos.

After each of these nightmares (I never knew on first waking that they were merely dreams, and would only gradually realize this), I held onto Langhua tightly. Even then I wasn't completely convinced that these things hadn't really happened.

"Why must I have such dreams?" I asked him. "I wonder if they can be explained in terms of superstition?"

"Don't be so foolish. Everything has to be explained in scientific terms. You think that these dreams have a psychological basis, don't you? Well, where do those dreams come from? They're reflections of the material world. Feel your shoulders and see how cold they are. You're having nightmares because your shoulders are so cold!" He fell back asleep immediately, leaving me awake and feeling a strong draft coming from the ceiling and from under the bed; the tip of my nose and my ears felt frozen.

Just how much snow fell during that night's storm I'll never know, but I was sure we wouldn't be able to open the door the next morning. I remember Granddad telling me once that during years of really heavy snowstorms, you couldn't see the heads of children standing in the snow. Winds continued to beat against our window. A puppy whimpered out behind the house.

My thoughts turned from the freezing cold to hunger. We had no rice for tomorrow.

13

Frost Covered His Upper Lip

EVERY night he went out under the cold, clear rays of the moon. He had to walk five li to a house on a quiet, secluded street, where he taught middle-school Chinese literature to two students. This was a new occupation—actually, it wasn't so much an "occupation" as it was a means of earning fifteen yuan.

His ears were exposed to the cold, for the turned-up collar of his lined coat didn't even cover his chin. Each night he went out like that, and each night was colder than the one before.

The sounds of someone walking noisily through the snow grew louder. He had returned, bringing a load of snowflakes home with him. His pant cuffs were a solid white; his shoes were soaked halfway through.

"Is it snowing again?"

He didn't answer, as though he were angry with me. He removed his socks, which were filled with snow. I took them from him and beat them against the door, but only a few snowflakes fell to the floor. They were soaked through. So I held them over the stove to dry them out, and a foul odor gradually filled the room.

"Let's have breakfast a little later tomorrow morning. There's someone over in Nangang District who wants to study martial arts with me. We can eat when I get back." He said this without any emotion, keeping his voice very, very low. Maybe he was just trying to be more serious than usual, or maybe he was playing the matter down. I didn't know what to make of it.

He put on a pair of cloth slippers and went across the way to hold his martial-arts class.

"Hold on a second. Your socks are almost dry."

"I don't want to wear them."

"Why not? Don't forget about Miss Wang."

"What's Miss Wang got to do with anything?"

"Won't it look bad?"

"So what if it looks bad!" He went outside barefoot, not caring that Miss Wang might notice. There were actually two pretty girls in the Wang family.

He was really busy now: he would go out to Nangang early in the morning, then after he had returned and finished breakfast, he would be off to teach Chinese literature to his "disciple." Right after that he'd be out on the streets trying to borrow some money. After dinner, he had to teach martial arts again, followed by his class in middle-school Chinese literature.

When night came, he would sleep straight through, without waking up even once. I began to grow terribly lonely. During the days, I would sit quietly in the company of our furniture—I had a mouth, but no one to talk to, legs, but nowhere to go, hands, but nothing to do. I was just like a disabled person—I was so lonely! My view was blocked by the walls, so I couldn't even watch the sparrows outside the window—I couldn't see a thing. The window was covered by a thick coat of frost and snow like a layer of felt. This was "home": no light, no warmth, no sound, no color—a lonely home, an impoverished home, little more than a desolate outdoor square where not even weeds would grow.

I stood in the walkway just outside the window waiting for Langhua. I was very hungry.

The metal gate rattled. My nerves were so taut that the sound made me jump. The gate rattled again and again, as people who had nothing at all to do with me came and went. Wang Lin, with her high fur collar and matching high-heeled shoes that clicked with each step, swayed as she walked past me, totally self-satisfied and blessed with a full belly; she smiled and pointed her finger at me in a very frivolous manner. "Aha! Waiting for your Langhua again?" she asked. Just before she reached the wooden steps in front of her door, she added, "Every day he goes out and you wait for him. What a lovely couple you make!"

Her voice had a brittle quality in the cold air. Maybe this was typical of young ladies' voices. I quickly put her out of my mind; maybe I hadn't really seen or heard her at all. I probably would have reacted the same way even if I had been a man. My stomach growled.

The smell of food frying in soy sauce emerged from the Wangs' kitchen; I could smell it all the way over here. They were having fried noodles! Every time the spatula clanged against the side of the pan, it seemed to be saying to me, *I'm frying noodles. I'm frying noodles.*

I kept standing in the walkway. My feet ached from the cold; my nose was running. So I went back inside, closed both the outside and the inside doors, then sat quietly for a long time, not even sure what I was thinking about.

Wang Lin's second elder sister was on her way to the cold-storage room to get some food. I was outside dumping some dirty water, and so we met. We normally had little to say to one another and acted more or less like strangers. But this time she asked me, "Haven't you been to see the movie? This one's pretty good—it stars the actress Butterfly." Her long, dangling blue earrings never stopped dancing.

"No." The cold penetrated my dress and froze my bones!

"It's really a good one. They get married in the end, and everyone in the audience was trying to imagine how wonderful their lives together would be if the movie hadn't stopped where it did."

She walked me to my door, full of enthusiasm, and I could still see her earrings dancing in the air.

"Come in and sit for a while."

"No, I can't. We're about to eat!"

Langhua returned home, his upper lip covered with a layer of frost. Miss Wang had already walked a long way off, but both her earrings and her words continued to dance in the air: "Your honeymoon partner is back. Here he is!"

What a lonely, desolate home! He took a flatcake out of his pocket and gave it to me. Then he went out again, saying that a movie house was looking for someone to make posters, that he was going to give it a try.

"When will you be back? Can you at least tell me that?" I asked as I followed him outside. He was like a bird I'd been trying to catch for a long time, only to have it fly away as soon as I had it in my grasp. Disappointment and loneliness; I felt ready to collapse from hunger even though I was eating the flatcake. The

45

young ladies' earrings—the line of frost on his upper lip. The daughters in the family across the way went to see movies and wore earrings—my home, ah! my home.

14

The Pawnshop

"You go! You go pawn it! I won't do it!"

"Okay, I'll go. I don't mind going into a pawnshop; it doesn't scare me a bit. After all, I'm not doing anything wrong."

My new jacket. So new I hadn't even worn it. Now I was taking it to the pawnshop! I hesitated briefly before entering the pawnshop, remembering Langhua's insistent parting words to me about the price—I was to accept nothing less than two yuan.

I placed the bundle on the counter, which I could reach only by standing on my tiptoes and stretching my body as much as possible. I never could figure out why pawnshop counters had to be so high!

The man in the skullcap looked the jacket over, and before he even opened his mouth, I said, "Two yuan."

He must have thought I was out of my mind; why else would he have rolled the bundle up without even giving me a passing glance, making as though to toss it back at me in obvious impatience?

"Well, if two yuan is too much, how much is it worth?"

"To me, nothing." He shook his melon-shaped head, which put into motion the little red ball on the top of his cap.

I fearlessly reached out to retrieve the bundle, confident that I had carried out my part of the bargain. I knew that he was just trying to give me a hard time, and all I wanted to do was retrieve my bundle and leave. I was right—he wouldn't let go of the bundle.

"Fifty cents! The sleeves on this jacket are too narrow. I'll have trouble selling it."

"No sale," I said.

"Okay, one yuan—but that's my final offer. Take it or leave it." He sort of leaned back. The counter was too high for me to see his protruding belly. He was wagging a stubby raised finger.

I left in a hurry with a one-yuan bill in one hand and a pawn ticket in the other. I felt quite refreshed as I walked along, considering myself to be a person of means. I stopped at the marketplace and the rice shop, emerging in no time at all with an armload of things. Even though the air was so cold that my hands ached, I didn't mind carrying so much; I felt that it was my duty. I had no sympathy for my hands, since their only function was to serve me; I might not have had any regrets if they had dropped off from the cold. I passed by a shop that sold meat-filled dumplings, went in and bought ten of them, then felt a surge of pride as I looked at myself carrying all these things. The adrenalin was really flowing, and I had no sympathy at all for my freezing, aching hands. As I walked by an old beggar on the street, I handed him a copper coin; I felt that since I had food to eat, he should have some, too. But I didn't give him too much, just a single copper coin. I had to keep the rest for my own use. I felt my pocket to make sure the pawn ticket was still there, then headed off toward home again. My hands were aching so much I had no thoughts for anything else. I must be nearly home. I must be nearly there. My spine was soaked with sweat, my legs were getting rubbery, and my eyes were stinging by the time I arrived at the front gate. Just then I realized that this marked the first time I'd been out of our room since moving there. My strength ebbed away; even the sun's rays struck fear into me.

I felt the pawn ticket in my pocket one last time before walking into the courtyard. Langhua was still in bed, just as he had been when I left. A pawnshop was one place he couldn't bring himself to enter. What was he thinking? As I handed my packages to him, he jumped to his feet.

"I'm starved! I was wondering if you'd ever come home!"

He waited until he had eaten most of the ten dumplings before asking, "How much did you get? You weren't cheated at the pawnshop, were you?"

After I handed him the pawn ticket, he looked at the small amount of money the thing was worth and said, "Only one yuan. Not enough."

He complained about the amount I had settled for at the pawnshop, but that didn't stop him from eating the dumplings. So in the end, he was satisfied. His mouth appeared much larger than the dumplings he had stuffed into it; one by one they went, until there were no more.

15

Borrowing

THE front gate of the Girls' Middle School, the very school where I had been a student three years earlier. It hadn't changed: the windows, the trees in front of the windows, the low slat fence, the street beyond the fence—I had, at one time or another, trod upon every stone step there. Every single tree, on both sides of the fence, carried memories for me. The neighboring houses called out to me with sentiments of bygone days.

I couldn't forget any of this! It didn't matter if the memories were sweet or bitter ones. I couldn't forget. Not any of it! Right there—upstairs—was where I had spent my youth.

Now it was dusk, dusk in the wintertime. I walked very gingerly up the concrete steps. The doorbell that I had pressed three years earlier was once again under my finger. The custodian who came out to answer the door recognized me. Young students running up and down the stairs cocked their heads as they asked one another, "Who's she looking for?"

It was all so familiar: the office signs, the mailbox, the telephone room—even the coat rack that had been there three years ago was still standing in the same place, just outside the reception room door.

I couldn't make myself walk up the stairs right away—I felt it would be somehow humiliating. Although some of the old students were still around, I was afraid that the classrooms might have been moved, and I didn't know if the dormitory was now upstairs or downstairs.

"Is Mr. Liang—Mr. Liang, the literature teacher—in school?" I asked the custodian.

"Yes, but right now he's in a teachers' meeting."

"When will it be over?"

"Not till seven o'clock, I'm afraid."

I looked up at the clock on the wall. It wasn't even five o'clock yet. No sense in waiting. As I walked out through the school gate, my feelings had changed completely. Paving stones, trees—what did any of them have to do with me?

"Hey! Over here!" Langhua was standing under a distant streetlight calling to me.

"Let's go home! Come on!" I walked up to him but said nothing more.

We had walked a long way down the inclined road before I told him what had happened:

49

"Mr. Liang was in a teachers' meeting, which won't be over till seven o'clock. How could we wait that long?"

"Can you walk? Does your stomach still hurt?"

"No, it's okay."

A full moon was rising in the east from behind a grove of trees—a dark orange moon, looming large and very turbid. It hung on the sky's edge like an old man's blurred eye. Our feet kept slipping on the snow-covered ground and made crunching sounds. We walked on and on, not seeing another person on the road until we had reached the train station. The station clock shone brightly through the darkness that was closing in. A train whistle shattered the cold night air. Streetcars, trains, horse-drawn carts, rickshas—the station was alive with them.

We walked parallel to the streetcar tracks, as one streetcar after another passed by us, their bells ringing loudly. We couldn't ride, since we hadn't been able to borrow any money, so we just kept walking. We walked shoulder to shoulder. I couldn't tell him that my stomach was hurting. As we crossed the bridge, the smoke from a passing train beneath us—probably eastbound—rose to meet us; the bridge rattled so much our ears rang. Steeling ourselves, we continued trudging ahead toward town.

After we reached the top of the hill, we looked down way off into the distance. The red and green electric lights in front of the shops seemed to be blinking on and off, and people on the streets seemed enveloped in a layer of haze as night fell. But for the light seeping out through the windows of their homes, all those buildings would have appeared so secluded and lonely, like great churches minus the sounds of church bells! From our vantage point on the top of the hill, the street-lights on Duke Xu Road looked like a string of yellow bronze bells that could reach all the way up to the sun;

the bells got closer and closer together the farther away they were, until we could no longer even count them!

We walked shoulder to shoulder, almost in a daze. The night, the city; it was all one huge sewer, a sewer in which we were caught up. We held hands. We pulled one another along. The night air was so cold, the ground so slippery, that I was always on the verge of stumbling. My legs were so shaky I seemed to have lost control of them. Eventually I did slip and fall in front of a movie house. I just sat there on the icy ground—the ground all around me was covered with ice—aware that I had hurt my knee. Even though he helped me to my feet and pulled me along, I could barely walk.

"Did you hurt your belly in the fall? You really can't walk, can you?"

After we returned home, I used what rice was left to make a pot of gruel. With no salt, no oil, no vegetables, all we could do was warm our stomachs a little.

But even that didn't help. We heated some water and poured it into a cookie tin, but it leaked. Langhua tried to fill a glass bottle with the hot water, so that I could drink it and warm up a bit, but as soon as he poured it in, the bottom of the bottle fell off, spilling the contents all over the floor. He picked up the bottomless bottle and blew into it like a horn. With the tooting sound from the bottle ringing in my ears, I lay down on the ice-cold bed.

16

Buying a Fur Cap

DARK tents had been raised at the flea market, covering a huge plot of ground, one almost on top of the other. Vendors' stalls were set up all over, offering every imaginable useful object for sale: shoes, socks, caps and hats, facecloths. There were more men's pants and shirts than anything else. One look at Langhua and I knew that I should buy him a pair of pants. But just as I was about to ask the price, my attention was caught by a row of fur-lined overcoats of different sizes, hanging on a rack high overhead: they had wide collars trimmed with black fur, and even though they were the type worn by carters and such, it seemed to me that Langhua would look just fine in one of them. Once again I was about to ask the price when Langhua called over to me, "Here, what do you think of this cap?" He held up his fist, on which sat a cap with four earflaps. He turned around to face me, and as soon as I saw the cap, which resembled a cat's head, I broke out laughing. "That's no good!" I said as I walked up to him.

"This is the only kind of cap I ever wore as a child back home." He put it on to see how it fit and was immediately transformed into a kitten. "It sure is warm." He turned down the two sideflaps and immediately became a puppy. With that cap on his head, he was a kitten or a puppy. It seemed like that to me because, when I was a child, Granddad had once given me one of these "Pekingese-dog caps"—that's what he had called them, "Pekingese-dog caps!"

"Boy, is this cap warm!" He put it back on his fist, turned it around once more, and shook it a couple of times.

The tent was so cold inside that my feet began to

ache badly, so we walked around while he tried on just about every aviator cap he saw. The black ones were twenty cents cheaper than the brown ones. He preferred the brown ones but liked the idea of saving twenty cents, so we held off and kept looking among the other stalls.

"Your—what want?" a man behind one of the stalls asked us. He was a Chinese himself, but assumed that all the other Chinese were Japanese or Koreans.

We couldn't buy any of his stuff, so we hurried past.

Langhua tried on one of the aviator's caps. Two large fur earflaps were covered by two smaller ones.

"Come on. Let's get going." We wound our way past a lot of stalls before emerging from the tent area. If he hadn't called me, I don't think I could have torn myself away from all the shirts and pants and, especially, the goatskin overcoats worn by carters.

As soon as I was outside again, I quickly caught up with him.

"How much money do we have left?"

"Fifty cents."

We walked past the food market, and I almost urged that we go into the little café where we used to eat and buy some meat-filled dumplings. But I held back when I thought again of our last fifty cents, putting the thought out of my mind and forcing myself to walk past the café. Fifty cents had to last us three days, so cafés were out of the question.

There were a lot of peddlers alongside the road selling peanuts and melon seeds.

"Do you have any change?" I tugged on his sleeve.

"Nope, none at all."

"Then, that's that."

"What do you want to buy?"

"Nothing."

"If you want something, what's wrong with using this bill?" He stopped walking.

"I thought I might buy some melon seeds, but if we don't have any change, I'll do without."

He was probably thinking: *What kind of man am I if I can't even satisfy my lover's wish to buy a few coppers' worth of melon seeds!* So he fished around eagerly in his pocket.

But this wasn't the time to be buying one's lover some melon seeds. Eating a real meal was far more important than eating a few melon seeds. Hunger is more important than a lover.

We walked the rest of the way home amidst swirling snowflakes. My hands ached. My feet ached. The whole trip had been a waste of time.

17

The Ad Man's Dream

A FRIEND of ours had found a job at a movie house painting ad posters for a monthly wage of forty yuan. The idea of painting movie posters had left a deep impression on me, and as I cooked breakfast, I scanned the want-ad section of the newspaper. I spotted an ad for another movie house looking for someone to paint posters, which sent my blood pumping. Why not me? Hadn't I studied art in school? But the ad didn't mention wages.

Langhua returned, and while we were eating breakfast, I told him of my plan. He opposed the idea. "That's just a trick," he said. "There was an ad in yesterday's paper for a tutor, so I went over to check it out. You've never seen so many people. Ten or twenty people had shown up to apply for a single job."

"Why are you afraid even to go see? If it's no good, we can just forget about it."

"Not me."

"If you won't go, I will."

"By yourself?"

"By myself!"

The next morning I kept an even sharper eye out for the ad, and this time I was even more pleased with what I saw: the ad had been changed to include the wages—forty yuan a month. There it was in black and white: forty yuan.

"Let's go take a look. If we don't, do you think a job's going to come looking for us?" I asked him.

"If you want to go, make it after breakfast. I've got something else to do." He was starting to weaken.

We met a friend of his on the way.

"Where are you headed?"

"To answer an ad for a movie-poster painter."

"Was that the one in the *International Gazette*?"

"That's the one."

"Forty yuan!" He had noticed it also.

The clock high atop the big store at the intersection showed that it wasn't even eleven o'clock. They weren't accepting applications until noon.

We looked for the place until we were exhausted. We had just about given up when we spotted the "office" where applications were being accepted. The ad had said that it was on a paved street, but it was actually on a little dead-end lane that paralleled the paved street. By then our eyes were already a bit dazzled. We entered the office, which was on the second floor of a large building. We noticed a shiny bronze rectangular sign hanging above the passageway, but before we could even see clearly just what kind of office this was, someone called us to a halt, "What do you want?"

"We're here to apply for the ad job."

"Today's Sunday. We're not open for business."

Luckily, our courage to go back hadn't left us by the next day. It was an overcast day, with snowflakes swirling in the air. The man at the office told us, "Go over directly to the movie house to apply for the job, please, since we don't do that here anymore."

Langhua grumbled at me as we walked out, "This is all your idea. I told you it was a trick, but you wouldn't believe me!"

"Why are you getting mad at me?" I was as angry as he.

"It's all because you wanted to be in the ad-painting business. Well, you go ahead and do it!"

That led to an argument. He felt it was all my fault; I felt he had no right to get mad at me. As we walked on, he led the way, with me a step or so behind. Apparently, he didn't want to walk alongside me. It seemed he was upset with me because I was always misjudging things. And so the dispute grew and grew, and neither of us directed any of our anger at the office or the movie house. He was angry only with me, I was angry only with him, and we both lost sight of the original cause. It soon turned into a shouting match.

I refused to go the third day, and I didn't bring up the subject again. All I did was warm my hands over the stove. He went out alone, wearing his aviator's cap.

"I won't be teaching martial arts to that guy in Nangang any longer," he told me that night.

I had known that fellow was no longer interested in taking lessons.

The next morning he put on his aviator's cap and went out, staying away the whole day. That night I continued to avoid the issue of the ad job. Nor did I bring up the subject the next day, for I no longer had any interest in finding that kind of work. But he had gone over there on his own—he had been paying more attention to the opportunities than I. He had twice gone by himself to the movie house.

"I went there twice. The first time they said the manager wasn't in, and the next time they told me to come back in a couple of days. Damn them! What's the big deal! It's only forty yuan, and for that I'd have to play their silly games! What kind of posters do you suppose they want painted? Dens of iniquity, lurid romances, sweetness and light, that's what! Nothing but a bunch of shameless and disgusting scenes!"

I didn't respond to his outburst. His temper was getting the better of him; it was as though someone were forcing him to become an ad man.

"Do you think that sort of stupid work is what we should be doing? Shit! The bastards!" The curses really started coming then, and he turned his anger on himself: "What a dumb bastard I am! A shameless piece of garbage. A selfish reptile!"

The incident was still on his mind at bedtime, for he said to me, "If you don't think we're a couple of selfish reptiles, then what are we? All we're concerned about is that we might starve, so we go out and paint movie posters, and we paint them well. So what if they're disgusting! We lure a few extra people to watch those torrid romances, encourage them to hanker after luxury, goad them into moving up and up—all that just because we're afraid of starving. Never mind how many people we're corrupting—people are no damned good! If someone were willing to pay two hundred yuan a month, is there anything we wouldn't do? If we can't push history ahead, at least we shouldn't stand on the opposite side and use what strength we have to turn history on its ear!" I was moved by his words, which got louder and louder as he spoke, even though he wasn't aware of it. He had begun the process of close self-analysis.

"Lower your voice a little. Our landlord often has Japanese guests," I said.

Another day had come, which we spent just walking around Central Avenue. The tall, skinny Lao Qin patted him on the shoulder. It was winter, so by three or four in the afternoon, dusk was already falling. What little sunlight remained hung atop the buildings, gradually losing its strength. The streets were already being buffeted by night winds. Gusts of snow- and frost-laden winds were already swirling around the feet of pedestrians on the sidewalks.

Whenever people met on the street during the winter, they shook hands without taking off their gloves. This fellow's gloves must have been really cold, because as soon as Langhua shook hands with him with his bare hand, he drew it right back. I looked down at Lao Qin's boots, which were dotted with globs of red and green.

"Why do you have paint all over your boots?"

He said he'd been painting posters over at the movie house. He pointed the place out to us: "They really keep me busy. I get off my regular job at four o'clock and have to be there by five. How about giving me a hand!"

Neither Langhua nor I answered him.

"I'll be waiting for you at the ticket booth at five o'clock. You'll spot me as soon as you enter." Lao Qin walked off.

Almost every one of the roasted flatcakes we ate for dinner that night was undercooked, but we ate them anyway. We were in such a hurry that we didn't even sit at the table, preferring to eat our dinner standing around the stove. The heat from the stove turned his face a bright red. As I stood there eating, I looked at the watch we had just bought. It was five o'clock, so we hurried off without even putting the cover on the pot; steam rose from the broth inside.

Naturally, I hadn't taken a single mouthful of soup. Langhua was already out the door ahead of me, so I followed after him, adjusting my cap as I hurried along.

Just as I'd run through the main gate, I suddenly re-called a stack of kindling beside the stove. Fearing it might catch fire, I ran back to take a look, and by the time I had made the round trip to the gate, he was al-ready at the intersection.

All he could say was, "You don't even know how to cook a fast meal! You just fumble around, and now we're late! All women know how to do is fumble around, and, boy, are they good at that!"

What a laughable contradiction. Wasn't this the very job he would have none of? Then why was he in such a hurry? He rushed into the movie house ahead of me. He was such a mass of contradictions that the back of his head itself seemed to be a contradiction. I was nearly laughing as I followed him in.

A man with a big nose—I couldn't tell if he was a Russian or an Englishman—was in the ticket booth sell-ing tickets. When we asked for Lao Qin, he said he didn't know him. We would have asked someone else, but we couldn't tell who was an employee and who wasn't. A half hour passed and still no Lao Qin. All we could do was return home.

As soon as we were home, out came his theories, as always: "God damn it! It was all your idea to go. No good. No good at all! It's a good thing for this selfish being we call man to bang his head against a few walls."

He left to go somewhere, leaving me at home alone.

"Why didn't you look around a little?" Lao Qin asked me as he took off his fur cap.

"Look where? We waited there for half an hour with-out seeing a trace of you!"

"Let's go there together? Where's Langhua?"

"He went out."

"Let's you and I go there first. You can be my helper. Forty yuan a month. Twenty for you and twenty for me, right down the middle."

I stood in front of the marquee until ten o'clock before going home. Langhua had been out looking for me twice without any luck, so he had come home and fumed.

We stayed up half the night arguing. He went out and bought some wine, half of which I drank. We cried. Both of us cried. While he was drunk, he lay on the floor and shouted, "As soon as you see a job, you forget everything else and take off! The minute you have a job, you don't even want your lover anymore!"

Was I such a terrible woman, one who would cause her lover to roll around angrily on the floor for a measly twenty yuan? The heart of a person who's drunk is like a burning flame, like boiling water; I didn't know why I was crying, for by then I was beyond reason. So was he.

When we awoke the next day after our binge, it was Sunday. He went along with me to spend the day painting movie ads. I was Lao Qin's helper, and Langhua was mine.

We didn't go the day after that, because the movie house had hired someone else.

We had actually realized our dream of becoming ad men, but then the dream was shattered.

18

New Acquaintances

So very lonely—everyone in Northern China was feeling very lonely. A group of us organized a painting club—I think the idea had been mine. We also organized a drama troupe. More than ten people attended the first meeting in the reading room of the People's

Education Hall, where we discussed the work of the drama troupe. One of the attendees had a pale face and looked a little like a government man; in the afternoon we adjourned to his home to continue the discussion. Not in ages had I been in a warm house such as that, with wall furnaces producing plenty of heat and the sun's rays shining in on my head. The bright, warm house made me feel hot all over!

The following day was a holiday, so we all went back to the man's home. We went in the evening, when the light from inside shone through the glass a frosty white. The people inside were moving around spiritedly, and there were occasional outbursts of loud-pitched laughter. Apparently no one had heard our knocks at the door. We knocked louder, but still no one heard us. Finally we went over and knocked on the window pane; a gray shadow appeared behind the gauze curtain. Whoever it was used his finger to wipe clean a spot on the frosted glass, then looked through the spot to see us. This was followed by the sound of someone in the hallway.

"Hey, everyone, Langhua's here!" Our host opened the door and light-heartedly shook hands with us.

Even though we hadn't known him long, he treated us as though we were old friends. We took off our overcoats there in the hallway; coats hung from nearly every hook on the coatrack.

"We're late!"

"Not that late! Not all that late! Not everyone's here yet!"

The table lamp in the living room had been lit. At the moment, people were sitting around the lamp reading scripts of plays. One of my former schoolmates was reading a script as she sat with her back to the wall furnace. The wall behind her was a pale yellow, and her back was outlined by a faint glow. Her black, permed hair hung nearly to her shoulders. She was reading the script as though she were auditioning for a part. With her wavy hair and rounded shoulders outlined by the pale yellow glow behind her, she looked like a papercut silhouette of a lovely young woman.

She stopped reading as soon as she laid eyes on me. The two of us sat there, our backs to the wall as we talked about everything under the sun. We studied and commented upon an oil painting that hung in a large frame. My feet, which were nearly frozen, began to itch as they warmed up inside my boots. But that was my problem, and I'd just have to put up with it!

Everyone in the living room was a stranger to me. They were all drinking tea and nibbling on melon seeds, while our host walked back and forth, looking every bit the part. He spoke very cordially, treating everyone with the utmost respect. He was constantly straightening his coat, sticking out his chest, and smoothing down his sleeve. I don't know how many times he straightened his bow tie, but everything he did made him look like the perfect host.

There were doors in every corner of the living room, which connected it to three other small rooms; the fourth door opened onto the hallway. A woman in a fur coat walked into the room through one of the doors, then she turned and walked right back out.

As I sat there reading a script under the lamp, I could hear Langhua speaking with someone in hushed tones. I looked up and saw that he was talking to a fat, military-looking fellow standing across from him. They walked over to the center of the living room and sat down alongside a round coffee table. I couldn't understand what they were talking about: they were saying such things as "Second Artillery Regiment," "the ninth period, eighth period," and talking about people I didn't know. Langhua mentioned a name I had never heard, and the other fellow repeated the name. It was all very mysterious, and I wasn't the only one intrigued by this unfamiliar terminology; everyone in the room grew quietly serious.

A young woman walked into the room through the door on the right. Even though she was wearing high-heeled shoes, she still looked like a little "Mongol" girl. The fat man stood up and said, "This is my woman!"

Langhua called me over and introduced me the same way, which gave me the opportunity to sit down beside them and listen carefully to their conversation.

As we were walking home, Langhua told me, "He was a schoolmate of mine."

Streetcar bells rang out continually, sparks danced as the streetcars passed by, a half moon rose in the western sky, the lamplight from the bean-milk stand on a streetcorner looked like a firefly's light, and the lonely vendor walked round and round as the bean milk in the pot cooled. It was late at night—very, very late.

19

"Ox Tether"

WITHIN three days our drama troupe broke up. A huge stack of scripts was still piled upon the table, giving me the feeling that the room had gotten larger and colder.

"They've been here already. I told them it's no good having such a crowd of people coming and going here all the time. The Japs have arrested a lot of workers in Outer City over the past few days. Take a drama troupe like ours—even if we're only a drama troupe, we'd have a lot of explaining to do if the Japs found out about it."

So now what? The drama troupe was disbanded, of course, so we stood up to go, since there was no longer any reason to stick around. It was saddening news. But

Langhua's fat friend went out and bought some melon seeds, so we sat back down and nibbled on the seeds.

We heard noises coming from the kitchen, which meant it was nearly dinnertime. We got up to leave, but they said, "Stay and eat with us! Don't leave. You don't have to be formal with us."

"No thanks, and we're not being formal—honest!" But we really were. Our fat friend's woman (the one I had characterized as a little "Mongol" girl) tried to bar my way from leaving.

"We've already eaten. Really we have!" We rushed out, playing a trick on our own stomachs. We both had an empty feeling, now that the drama troupe had been disbanded. We walked along listlessly.

"What a waste of time! We went over there all those times for nothing. I've got a headache!"

"Hurry up! Don't walk so slowly!" Langhua said.

Actually, more than the matter of the drama troupe was trying my patience—I was hungry! And I knew there wasn't a single thing to eat at home.

Since we had no place else to go, we often returned to the man's home to sit and pass the time. Our fourth visit fell on New Year's Eve. We'd been invited to celebrate New Year's there, and all of our new acquaintances were glad to have us around to join in on the festivities.

"It seems that "Ox Tether" has captured a couple more oxen!" someone said.

This was met with laughter that mystified me. What was the significance of "Ox Tether"? I hadn't a clue.

"During the summer we planted some 'ox tether' flowers [morning glories] in front of the window, but we planted so many that they wound up covering the entire window! That's why we call the place 'Ox Tether,' " our host explained to me in a loud, laughing voice.

But why call people "oxen"? I didn't know them well enough to actually ask this question, but it was on my mind.

No matter how light-hearted and noisy we were, everyone did exactly what was expected. The maid went out to buy some pine seeds, taking thirty cents with her. As though my own money were being spent, I couldn't help thinking it was being wasted. I was so anxious I nearly began to tremble! It was as though the maid were throwing the money away. *That's not necessary! You don't have to do that! Why eat pine seeds? Don't eat them! Don't eat useless things like that!* Again, I didn't actually say anything—this was neither the time nor the place. That much I knew. Later on, even though I ate my share of seeds, I didn't savor them like everyone else. They were eating the seeds as a snack; I was eating them to satisfy my hunger! So I ate one after another, swallowing them without even pausing to enjoy their flavor.

I didn't let Langhua in on this silly secret of mine until we were back home. He told me he'd also eaten quite a few of the pine seeds without even being aware of it. Like me, he had eaten them as though they were a meal.

The fact that the two of us had shared nearly identical feelings surprised me at first. It shouldn't have. For both of us, the same hunger had forged our feelings.

20

A Ten-yuan Bill

PEOPLE were dancing and having a grand time under the greenish light; some were actually dancing with chairs. Even our fat friend put his accordion aside and twisted and wove his way into the crowd of people. But he didn't blend in with the others, partly because he was so fat and partly because he had such a funny way of dancing. His uncoordinated legs were twisting so violently they seemed spastic. He kept bumping into other people—intentionally—and finally succeeded in moving everyone off the floor, leaving him all alone—a fat, sweaty man, totally unconcerned that he was being laughed at.

"The old ox really knows how to bounce!" someone shouted.

But he ignored the comment. He wasn't dancing—he was just leaping around crazily, making a complete mockery of dancing. He was as clumsy as a pig or a crab.

A red lamp was lit, turning the twisting, dancing green people into red ones. The effect the red light had on the people was quite different: their enthusiasm over their crazed dancing increased. Tall, skinny Lao Tong made himself up like a lady and danced with our fat friend. We women laughed until tears streamed down our cheeks! We were doubled over with laughter! But our fat friend kept right on twisting and turning. And his "female" partner moved right along with him, twisting her head back and forth, putting on an uninhibited and unsightly show, twisting and turning until her head was nearly wrenched out of place and her hips seemed about to come out of their sockets. She kept on, seemingly shameless, her rouged, lipsticked face contorted with a grotesque smile that seemed to cover her entire face!

The next time Lao Tong left the room to make himself up, he returned with a red bandana wrapped around his head and a stiff but not completely inflexible handle sticking out from behind his neck; it was a piece of red cloth, twisted tight as a broom handle. He started dancing again, and his every movement made the "tail" bounce up and down.

Once the dancing ended, everyone ate apples and candy and drank some tea. But it wasn't at all like real eating! Someone said, "I can swallow an apple whole!"

"I'll bet you can't! If you can swallow an apple whole, then I can swallow a live pig whole," someone challenged him.

Naturally, neither an apple nor a pig was swallowed.

The chain that tethered the dog belonging to the family in the house directly opposite began to rattle. The December moon grew cold. The freezing dog began to whimper.

The colored lamp was put out, and the people, losing the stimulus of color, quieted down. I suddenly felt tired after all that excitement. Maybe everyone else did, too, for they quieted down, regaining their human characteristics. One of the little patrol vehicles we called "iron donkeys" came down the street, tooting as it passed by: the Japanese MPs were making their rounds! But no one was frightened. We didn't know very much about Japanese MPs.

"Have a good time! Enjoy yourselves!" said the first man to get to his feet.

"If we don't, we've only ourselves to blame. 'Today we have wine, so today we get drunk,' " said Lao Tong, the tallest among us.

Our fat friend's woman handed me a letter.

"Read this when you get home," she said.

Langhua walked up alongside me but had no idea

what was going on. I slipped the letter into my pocket.

The cold wind slapped us in the face the moment we stepped outside. We raised our collars. I could see that Langhua's coat was too thin to keep out the cold, but he said, "I'm not cold."

The people walked out, commenting that they had had more fun during the lunar New Year's gathering, that the euphoria had long since died away. I was feeling hungry, but what was there to eat at home? I no longer paid any attention to what the others were saying. Langhua must have been cold, for he took hold of my arm and started walking ahead, going faster and faster, until we had put quite a distance between us and the others.

Even though my feet ached, I sat down to read the letter by candlelight. When I opened it, a ten-yuan bill fell out.

The night was so quiet, the puppy out back was whimpering.

Some friends came by the next day, inviting us to join them for dinner over at "Ox Tether." It was a fine meal—hunger-stopping meals like that came around all too infrequently. There was fish, meat, and a delicious soup. Once again we didn't return home until late at night, and on that night there was more spring in my step than usual. The thought of hunger didn't bother me, since a ten-yuan bill was waiting for me at home. I walked with a brisk stride, unaffected by the winds. New Town Street. Central Avenue. Not many people were on the streets. The few who were walked along the icy roads like unshod horses, stepping gingerly as though they might slip and fall at any moment.

All the storefronts were closed and barricaded with steel gates; the stores themselves were darkened. Only the streetlights and a policeman remained. The policeman conveyed about as much authority as the trash bins on the sidewalks. Only the rifle slung over his back reminded us of his occupation; without it, I suspect he would have curled up beside an electric-wire pole and gone to sleep. We were just a short way from Market Street, but for some reason I still felt like walking that night. The big clock on the façade of the Russian hotel looked very lonely. Ahead of us to the north, at the end of the street, was the Sungari River.

My boldness still had not deserted me by the time we turned onto Market Street. Ten-yuan bills were everywhere! In my head, in my heart, along my spine, on my legs. Because of that ten-yuan bill, I was nearly floating on air. I had to laugh at myself.

It was a beggar! He was on the other side of the street moaning. *I'll bet he doesn't have a ten-yuan bill!*

I unlocked the metal gate and walked into the courtyard, but still I could hear the moans of the beggar.

21

A Like-fated Fish

OUR little fish had died. It had jumped out of its bowl and had died on the floor.

I felt terrible remorse. Why had I stayed out so long! Why had I been so concerned with my own entertainment that I'd let our fish die out of water!

When I had put the fish on the basin to wash them that day, two revived, both of them righting themselves and flipping around in the water. So I cooked only the three dead fish for that evening's dinner. One by one the scales came off and sank to the bottom of the basin. The bellies were slit open and the innards slithered out. Since this was my first attempt at cleaning fish, I concentrated hard on the scaling—it was sort of an experiment, a frightening one at that. The icy cold fish reminded me of snakes, and I didn't have the nerve to gut them. So Langhua did it as I stood alongside and watched. Even at that, I shied away from the sight, just like an uneducated country girl who sees a dead cat and is afraid it might come back to life at any minute.

"Just see how useless you are, afraid even of a fish!" He put down the cleaned fish and set to work on the belly of the second. But this one suddenly twitched. I quickly grabbed him by the shoulder and shouted, "It's still alive! This one's still alive!"

"What do you mean, alive! You're too edgy. Just watch me!" He pushed down hard with the knife and slit the fish's belly. The fish lurched and jumped back into the water.

"Now what'll I do?" It was his turn to ask me. How was I supposed to know? He picked the fish out of the water, moving it around as though he were afraid it might bite him. Then he thrust it back into the water. Half of the fish's innards were swirling around in the water—it was dead now.

"Well, it's dead, so we might as well eat it."

The fish was back in his hand, lying motionless. He went back to work and calmly finished cleaning it. By the time he had cleaned the third fish, I was just standing alongside—not daring to watch but wanting to, nevertheless. The third fish had been dead, for sure, for it didn't so much as twitch. A smaller fish still in the water, however, was alive and lively; it kept trying to swim in the basin. The last one was also alive, but just barely—it would remain motionless for a while, then float stiffly to the surface.

The stovetop was hot. By the time my face felt uncomfortably warm, the oil in the pan was sizzling. The fish, ready for frying, were laid out on the chopping board. As I rushed to get some more oil from the bottle just inside the doorway, I could hear sounds coming from the kitchen behind me—splashes and loud slaps. He also came over to take a look. The fish in the basin were still swimming around. The ones on the chopping board were still alive, too! Or at least one of them was. Its tail was noisily slapping the chopping board!

I didn't know what to do. I hadn't the heart to look at that pitiful thing, so I tried to hide in the doorway. *We won't eat that one*, I thought to myself. But its innards were gone. How could it still be alive? Tears welled up in my eyes, and I simply couldn't look any longer. I turned and gazed out the window, where I saw the puppy chasing the chicken with the red feathers, and the landlord's maid Xiao Ju crying at the base of the wall, having suffered a beating.

What a cruel world! A world devoid of human feelings! A violent world bent on destruction! All these things that have lost their human feelings deserve to be destroyed!

We served up the fish for dinner that night, but it had such a fishy taste that we didn't eat much. We threw most of it into the garbage.

The two live fish continued to swim in the basin. After we went to bed at night, we were awakened by splashing sounds from the kitchen. We got up, lit a candle, and decided to go in and take a look. But I didn't have the heart, so Langhua went in alone.

"One of them's dead, but the other's still swimming around making lots of noise."

The next morning we wrapped the dead fish in newspaper and threw it into the garbage. Now only one was left swimming in the basin. I changed the water, and after breakfast I threw some kernels of rice into the water for it.

The fish passed two happy days but became melancholic by the third; several times I spotted it lying motionless at the bottom of the basin.

"The little fish isn't eating. It's probably going to die soon," I said to Langhua.

He flicked the rim of the basin with his fingernail, and the little fish twitched a couple of times. He flicked it once more, and the little fish twitched again. If he didn't flick the rim, the fish didn't move but just sank to the bottom.

Another day passed. There was no longer any movement in the fish's tail, not even if we flicked the rim of the basin.

"He'd be fine if we tossed him into the river. He wouldn't die. He's feeling so low because he's lost his freedom!"

"How could we do that? The river's still frozen, and even if we managed to find a break in the ice big enough to toss him back, he'd freeze to death. Either that or he'd starve," I said.

Langhua laughed, saying I was just like someone playing with a bird: after putting it into a cage, I'd feed it some rice and say that it had no worries, that it was better off than being out in the wild where it might freeze or starve to death.

"Who doesn't love freedom? The oceans love freedom; the wild beasts love freedom; insects love freedom." Langhua flicked the basin again.

Our fish was in the doldrums for only a couple of days before it perked up again; its tail began splashing the water. I watched it every day as I cooked at the stove, exactly as I would have done with a child of my own who had just gotten over a sickness, showing a little more concern and a little more love than usual. The weather was unbearably cold. I made up my mind to take it over to the river as soon as the cold weather passed.

We went over to our friends' home every night to have a little fun, leaving our fish to pass the nights alone in the kitchen in blissful ignorance. It feared nothing—neither that it might be snatched out of the water by a cat nor startled out of it by rats. When we returned home late at night, we looked in. Always it was swimming peacefully in the basin. We didn't have a cat, so we knew there was no danger.

Another night at our friends' home, a night of dancing and singing. We didn't return home until the following evening. We'd been gone too long, and our fish had died!

Langhua was the first to walk in the door. He nearly stepped on the fish. After lighting a candle, we could see that it was still breathing—its gills were still moving slightly. I bent down to feel its scales—they were all dry. When had our little fish jumped out of the water? In the middle of the night? At dusk? *Were you frightened by rats? Did you hear the mew of a cat?*

Wax from the burning candle dripped all over the floor. I raised the candle, unaware of how crookedly I held it.

Since the fish was still breathing, I picked it up off the floor and put it gently back into the water, almost as though I were performing a funeral rite. A heavy sadness descended upon me; my hand began to tremble.

Our ill-fated fish was dead! *Who caused your death? You were so young, you came to this world–let's say you'd been part of a school of fish–you were young, you should have had a chance to live and grow, but you died!*

Langhua went out, leaving me alone in the deserted room. The moment he opened the door on his way back in, I ran to meet him: "The fish, it isn't dead after all; it's still alive!" Tears welled up in my eyes as I clapped my hands. I walked over to the table to pick up the candle. He flicked the rim of the basin, but nothing happened. The fish didn't move.

"Why isn't it moving?" I dipped my hand into the water to right it, but it bellied up again.

"Get up. Watch the candle wax." He yanked me away from the basin.

The fish was really dead this time! But before long, it revived once more. This time we were sure that it wouldn't die after all. It had just been out of the water so long that it needed more time to recuperate, that was all.

Langhua got up in the middle of the night to take a look; he said that it wasn't moving, but not to worry. It was probably just asleep. I cautioned him not to move the little fish, that it needed lots of rest to get well. He was not to disturb it.

Sunrise came, and the fish was still asleep. We finished breakfast, and it was still asleep. I threw some more kernels of rice into the basin. I was careful to walk softly, so as not to make the floorboards tremble and startle the fish out of its sleep. As far as I was concerned, the fish was sleeping.

But it never woke up. I wrapped it in some newspaper. Its scales were bloodied and one of its eyes had been shattered, no doubt during its struggles on the floor.

I took it out to the garbage, and that was that.

22

A Few Carefree Days

THE people danced. Every night at "Ox Tether" the people danced. Over Lunar New Year's, they all gathered round a tea table, where they set up a big red candle and pretended to be paying their respects to the God of Wealth and worshipping their ancestors.

Lingqiu was wearing a purple satin gown under a yellow jacket, with a matching yellow sash around his waist. He was the first to kneel before the spirit table. Lao Tong performed his routine, putting on the tight-fitting cheongsam that belonged to Lingqiu's wife. It barely reached his knees. With his red face and the red cloth wound tightly into a broom-handle tail sticking out from behind his head, he knelt alongside Lingqiu. The two of them performed in unison, accompanying each kowtow with a sort of chant. One, two, three—just like punching dolls, they kept bobbing up and down, seemingly unable to stop.

The two of them built a small fire right on the floor, saying that since it was New Year's, they had to burn spirit money for the dead. They performed this skit so often that we became quite used to it. It didn't matter if it were New Year's or not. It was the same thing every day until the rest of us grew tired of it. We watched them with little enthusiasm and even less laughter. So they changed their act—they started playing hide-and-seek.

The living room was an ideal place for this new game. People scampered back and forth, hiding under the table, putting overturned chairs over their heads and running this way and that. In the process, one of the lightbulbs was sent crashing to the floor. The blindfolded "seeker" was teased and taunted by the "hiders." They'd tap him on his silly head, slap his groping arms, and make all sorts of noises to fluster him—croaking frogs, barking dogs, oinking pigs—even human sobs. Catching someone was no easy matter, for some of the people went through the doors into the small rooms. The blindfolded seeker would sometimes grope his way into one of the rooms and catch someone hiding behind the door. Once in a while the seeker would catch one of Lingqiu's children by mistake. But though he knew he might be entering one of the small rooms, he would blunder ahead anyway. One blindfolded man even groped his way up to Miss Wang's door.

"I wouldn't advise going into that room," someone was about to warn him.

"Just watch. Let's see what happens. Don't say anything!" someone else cautioned.

A stillness settled over the room, as though everyone were anticipating a noteworthy event. The "blind" man's hand touched the brass door knocker. He was all set to open the door, enter the room, and "catch" Miss Wang. We all had the same thought: *Let's see how he manages to catch her!*

"Who is it? Who's there? Come in please!" This was followed by a clicking sound as the door was opened to allow the guest to enter. She thought a friend was coming to call on her.

A wave of laughter engulfed the room as the blindfold was quickly removed. The blushing Miss Wang closed the door with a smile on her face.

Having grown tired of our game, we all sat down and had some tea. Our conversation somehow turned from pranks and nonsense to more serious matters. When the discussion got around to the issue of human conduct, our interest was at its peak: What was "human"? What was not?

"A person without emotions is not human."

"A person without courage is not human."

"Cold-blooded animals are not human."

"Cruel people are not human."

"Only people with human feelings are human."

Silence.

Everyone had his own definition of what was human. Some gave as many as two standards for determining what was human. At first we were seated, but people began rising to speak. Some even jumped to their feet.

"Man is an emotional animal. Without emotions there

can be no sympathy, and a lack of sympathy leads to selfishness, to a concern only for oneself—the result is mutual destruction, and that is not human." The speaker opened his eyes wide to show that he was on the side of reason. His expression indicated that he had given the ultimate and correct definition of being human.

"You're wrong. What's all this talk about sympathy! There's no such thing as sympathy. The Chinese are cold-blooded animals, so they're not human!" This rebuttal came from the first speaker, who stood up to deliver it. Since he seldom spoke, we paid close attention to his occasional pronouncement.

He was blushing with embarrassment by the time he had finished speaking. He was a native of Shandong, and Lao Tong responded by mimicking his Shandong accent: "Lao Meng, *wat* about you? *Ahr* you human?"

A lot of them liked to tease Lao Meng, mainly because he was such an honest, unpretentious fellow. They said he was like a young lady.

Lao Tong's nickname was "The Romantic Poet." He loved to drink, and he could toss off line after line of poetry without having to write it down—it just rolled off his tongue, seemingly without any thought. He wrote poems about virtually everything he saw, even the arrival of a friend:

Bang, bang, bang. Hear the door clang.
Who, pray tell, is there?

In a word, even if it were a fight between a dog and a cat, if someone asked him about it, out would come a poem. He had absolutely no interest in discussing the nature of humans or society! So he shied away from the tea table, where the rest of us were arguing about being "human," and picked up a book of Tang poetry, which he began to read aloud:

Yesterday . . .
Cannot be recaptured . . .
Today . . .
. . . so . . . vexing . . .

He read with feeling and expression, intent on disrupting the heated discussion around him. Langhua was just then loudly proclaiming, "Humans are those who neither exploit nor are exploited."

Lao Tong began to grow bored with his poetry reading: "Come on, let's go! Let's go get drunk." He noted that only Lingqiu showed any interest, so he added, "Come on, let's go! Let's get drunk. My treat."

By the time the treat was over and we had returned, all of us were pretty drunk. Langhua sang snatches of a song, over and over, a musical adaptation of Goethe's scene of separation between Werther and Lotte. It was well received by the rest of us, who tried to learn the words.

Someone began to sob. Just like Lotte herself, a young woman had been moved to tears by the song. Who wouldn't be? But who was it? It was Miss Wang. One of the young bachelors in the living room was also moved—not by the song, but by Miss Wang's crisp, enchanting sobs. The sound moved Fei to roll back and forth on the floor.

Lao Tong was listening more intently than anyone, his ears nearly standing straight up, his neck stretched longer than usual. He strolled over to the door to listen—then he said pointedly, "What're you crying about? How silly can you be!" In truth, there was nothing silly about how moved he himself had become. That's why he kept listening and why he kept saying, "Silly, really silly."

No more than a few days passed before Lao Tong and Miss Wang had fallen in love! Since the young lady was well known to us all, she joined us as we danced in the living room. From that time on, Lao Tong's monkey business took on more dignified airs!

He was too embarrassed to wear that piece of red twisted cloth on his head in front of Miss Wang, and whenever Lingqiu asked him to do one of his crazy dances, he would retort, "I don't dance!" His interest in the subject was nonexistent.

Miss Wang took a pink gauze veil out of her trunk and asked, "Who would like to be a young lady? I'll make him up."

"Here, me—I'll do it!" Now how could Lao Tong look like a young lady! He rushed over, looking like a giraffe.

He was very pleased with himself, for even though it was nothing but monkey business, at least it had a dignified air. He put the veil over his face, very neat and proper, then danced daintily around the room. But our feeling in watching him was exactly the same as when he had paraded around with the red cloth sticking out behind him like a broomstick!

The other bachelors began to envy lucky Lao Tong. But luck remained just beyond his reach, for the young lady had by then fallen in love with someone else!

So "The Romantic Poet" went back to composing poetry. It was then that he was robbed—someone stole his blanket. He commemorated this event by composing a poem entitled "Crying for My Blanket." This poem, in which he cried for his blanket, was one of his best. He added a new stanza every few days or so, and whenever one of his friends saw him, he would ask, "How goes the crying for your blanket?"

23

The Female Tutor

A LOWER-MIDDLE-SCHOOL student came to our home, books in hand, to take his lessons. Langhua conducted the class in such a loud voice that I hid in the kitchen. The same student returned the next day, but without his books, saying that his father wouldn't permit him to read modern, vernacular texts; he had plans for the boy to become a merchant, for whom vernacular texts were worthless. If he studied the classics, his father would pay his tuition, but if he studied vernacular texts, his father would wash his hands of him.

Just before he left, he took a one-yuan bill out of his pocket and handed it to Langhua.

"I'm very sorry, Teacher. I studied with you for a day, so here's one yuan!" He seemed very upset—it was obvious that he didn't want to become a merchant. As he held the bill in his hand, he was ready to cry.

It was a distressing scene for Langhua and for me, and before the boy walked out, we forced him to put the money back into his pocket.

Langhua's two other middle-school students also stopped coming.

He certainly wasn't cut out for this type of work. Now our means of livelihood was completely severed. Our fat friend had just recently moved, and I delivered a note to him that Langhua had written.

On the road back, I set out with rice, noodles, firewood, and a little spending money. I kept staring at the horse-drawn cart, afraid that the carter would run off with my firewood, and I was walking so fast that the rice in the cardboard box in my hands was shaking violently. I was also afraid that the bag of noodles on the cart would fall off, so I ran over and rearranged it.

Langhua didn't come out until he heard the tinkling of the horsebells. The sight of what I had brought with me really brightened his mood—he very lovingly carried the bag of noodles into the house. Then, clad only in a thin jacket, he began stacking the firewood in front of the window.

"Come in and warm up a little before you go outside again—it's freezing out there!" But I couldn't convince him to stop, and he didn't come inside until he had stacked all the wood.

"Boy, it's cold out there!" He was cupping his reddened ears with his hands.

He let out a puff of air and ran back outside. He wanted to start a fire in the stove—this would be the first time he had ever done that.

"That's a lot of firewood! Enough for five or six days at least! And there's enough rice and noodles for five or six days, too. Our worries are over!"

I washed the rice as he started the fire. He talked more spiritedly than he had in a long time, a result of seeing all that rice and noodles. But I just ignored him.

We ate the rice and noodles, morning and night. Before long it was gone, but it fed us right up to the time when I became a tutor.

Just like him, I spread a sheet of newspaper over the table and conducted class in a loud voice. I could barely keep from laughing when I saw him hiding in the kitchen. The girl, my student, was studying an elementary-school text—*pig, goat, dog,* and such words. I really didn't have to teach her. She would snatch the book out of my hands and say, "I know that one. I know it!"

Any time we ran across words she knew, she'd read them, one at a time. I could do nothing about it. The problem was, she was older than I, which was a little embarrassing.

She gave me five yuan at the beginning and said, "I'll give you five more in a few days."

Since she didn't show up for four or five days after that, I assumed she wasn't coming back. But she returned one night as I was cooking dinner. She said she'd been sick for several days, although she didn't look it. So why had she come back? After a considerable pause, she walked up next to me and said, "Teacher, I'd like to ask you a favor."

"What is it? Go ahead and ask." I dropped some chopped onions into the hot oil.

She was clutching a slip of paper in her hand; it was warm to the touch as she handed it to me. What was it? A prescription? A letter? No, it was none of those.

I tried to read it with the aid of a drippy candle alongside the stove, but it wasn't clear enough. I couldn't have read it if I lit a whole row of candles, since I didn't know the written characters.

"This is from the *Yijing*, the *Book of Divination*," Langhua announced after studying it for a long time.

"I had my fortune told, but no one I've talked to can understand what it says. I figured that since you were so learned, I'd bring it over and let you look at it."

After she left this time, she never returned. She must have figured that she could learn nothing from a teacher who didn't even know how to read a fortune!

24

Spring Appears on the Branches

MARCH! Flowers hadn't yet bloomed, so there was still no fragrance in the air. The accumulated muddy snowdrifts on the road were just beginning to melt and dry. The skies grew hazy, filling up with spring clouds. Warm breezes wafted veil-like over the streets and the courtyards. People north of the Great Wall don't feel the arrival of spring until the end of the season.

Spring had arrived: buds appeared on the white poplars that lined the streets, steam rose from the nostrils of the horses that pulled the carts, the carters' felt boots were no longer to be seen, and the legs of foreign women out walking, which had recently been covered up by their high boots, reappeared. The sounds of laughter, of people shouting greetings to one another, were once again heard on the sidewalks.

Doing their part quickly to enhance the feeling of spring, the merchants decorated their storefront windows with blooming flowers and lush grasses, producing one summer scene after another. I stood there, entranced by the sight, when someone bumped me. It was Wang Lin. She was wearing a hat with a narrow brim.

"It's so warm out! You can get hot just from walking!"

I followed her with my eyes as she turned the corner toward Market Street. We walked up to another store front; we weren't planning on buying anything, just window shopping and soaking up some sun. It was such a nice sidewalk, lined with trees and benches all along the way. We sat on a bench and closed our eyes, completely absorbed in spring dreams, spring fantasies, spring warmth.

Listen, listen! It's the song of spring!

"Master, Mistress—help me, please!—" What sort of spring song was that? It was coming from somewhere behind us.

That's not the song of spring!

The beggar was eating a rotten pear. One of his legs was so swollen, all the way down to his foot, that the other one didn't even seem to exist.

"My leg's frozen! Master, please help me! Ai, ai!"

Who could still remember winter! The sun's rays were so warm! Buds were sprouting on the roadside trees!

The song of a concertina came to us from the next street over. But it wasn't the song of spring. How sad the blind man made us as he cocked his head and played his concertina. The blind man couldn't experience spring, for he had no eyes. The man with the swollen leg couldn't walk in the spring, and he might as well have had no legs at all.

There's no reason for the world's unfortunate people even to be alive! They should be exterminated as soon as possible, so that the rest of us need never listen to the horrible song they sing!

Wang Lin was in the middle of the courtyard smoking a cigarette. She had changed into a pale green dress the same color as the buds on the trees. She had a letter tucked up under her arm, which she quickly stuffed into her pocket when she saw us.

"I'll bet it's another love letter!" Langhua said teasingly.

She ran into her room, leaving behind a wisp of smoke from her cigarette, which swirled in the air for a moment then disappeared.

Evening, a spring evening, an evening when Central Avenue was filled with the sounds of music: the music of vagrants, music from the Japanese dance halls, music from the foreign restaurants.

A little past seven in the evening. The middle of Central Avenue. An intersection. The crisp, loud sounds of a radio nearly filled the air above the street. If one stood in front of a storefront window, one might suspect that the sound came from the glass itself. For the first time this wide avenue, which had been so lonely in the wind and snow, had called out to us.

Foreigners, gentry, vagrants, old women, young ladies—the street was jammed with people. Some were crowding around storefronts, nearly obscuring them, but these were all young people. Others were singing songs, like so many gramophones, but these, too, were nearly all young people. It was an unusual sight— gatherings of young people. The young men were laughing and talking with young ladies, and all of them were walking together. The number of Chinese joining in with these curly-haired people was extremely small—no more than one in seven, or one in eight.

But Wang Lin was there. We ran into her. She was walking with a pale-faced woman who, like her, was beautifully made up. The curly-haired people told her in Russian that she was beautiful; she smiled and responded to them in Russian.

The crowds of people thinned at the southern end of Central Avenue.

Pitiful sobs emerged from the bases of walls and from out-of-the-way corners: old men, children, mothers— the sobbing people were society's perennial outcasts!

Over there, looking over there we could see the happy people. We could hear the happy songs coming from over there.

March. Flowers hadn't yet bloomed; people couldn't yet smell their fragrance.

The streets in the evening. The tender green buds on the branches hidden in the darkness. Was it winter? Autumn? But happy people were always happy, whatever the season. Sobbing people always sobbed, whatever the season.

25

The Carter, the Thief, and the Old Men

WE heard the rumbling sounds of the firewood cart as it came down the cobbled road. The old horse strained mightily to pull the cart as it left the lumber yard, piled high with our firewood. But there wasn't nearly enough to satisfy me. Compared to that gigantic pile at the yard, the firewood on this cart was like a single hair on the back of an ox. As far as I was concerned, the load seemed much too small.

"There're two pieces missing! A thief got them, can't you see that? You have to keep your eyes open! Thieves are always out to get firewood—you can lose as many as eight or ten pieces!"

The carter put me on my guard; I wasn't going to allow even a single piece to be taken. His words reminded me of the importance of firewood. Thieves were always on the lookout for available firewood.

"Here comes one!" the carter yelled, as a wild-looking thief appeared.

Langhua let out a scream, and the man with the ramrod-straight hair ran off.

"*Trash* like you doesn't know the meaning of the word shame! You got two pieces already. Why can't you be satisfied? Here, why don't I just hand the whole cart-ful over to you!" The carter flicked his whip in the air and railed at the thief without pause, haranguing him about "never being satisfied!"

We unloaded the cart in the center of the courtyard, piece by piece, but the carter had stopped helping us long before we had cleared it all off. When we handed him his money, he said to us, "Mister, how about giving me these last couple of pieces. I can take them back home with me and make a nice fire. My kids are small, and our place is so cold."

"Sure, take them with you!" I could see that five of the biggest pieces remained on the bed of his cart.

He bent over and started picking up splinters on the ground, tossing them, along with pieces of bark, up onto the bed of his cart. Then he walked off, leading the horse. Not a word about "never being satisfied' or any of the other things he had said. He just walked through the gate and out onto the street.

The sight of a firewood cart in the courtyard always drew a crowd of onlookers on the other side of the gate. "You need that firewood cut?"

They had their saws with them. Two oldtimers were pressed up against the gate.

We decided to let those two cut up our load of firewood. As soon as one of them saw that there was work, he turned to his partner and asked him, "Want somethin' to eat?"

I went out and bought some bread for them.

When they had finished cutting the wood, they stacked it in our woodshed. I didn't have a minute's peace all afternoon. I don't think I had ever experienced the sort of happiness that this pile of firewood brought me. I couldn't sit still, running out every few minutes to take a look. Finally the oldtimers swept the courtyard clean, and I paid them for their work.

I used splinters and bark to light the first fire. March evenings were still pretty cold, and the glass in the window was covered with steam. We didn't light the lamp, since sparks and flashes of light were coming from the fire I'd lit. When I opened the gate of the stove, the fire inside put a red glow on my face. I felt totally at peace.

I went outside to get some more bark and was shocked by what I found! The oldtimer was still there, his axe and saw thrown over his shoulder, while his partner was standing nearby with a wood-carrying pack on his back. Why were they still hanging around? They'd been there so long. Why didn't they leave?

"Didn't you give us too much money, Ma'am?"

"What do you mean, too much? No, I gave you the seventy-five cents you asked for, didn't I?"

"You didn't take out anything for the bread, Ma'am." The oldtimer hadn't yet put the money I had given him into his pocket; he was still holding it in his hand, counting it by the light of a distant lamp.

"You don't owe me anything for the bread," I said. "Keep what I gave you."

"Thank you, Ma'am." They turned and walked off, apparently very grateful, feeling that I had shown them a great kindness by not charging them for the bread.

My heart burned with a sense of shame. I watched the two oldtimers' retreating backs for the longest time, tears of remorse and sadness welling up in my eyes. They were my grandfather's age; how could they feel gratitude over a little bread?

26

The Park

THE edges of the pond were covered with gently swaying leaves. A slightly overweight man was crossing the footbridge—he was a newspaper editor.

"How long have you been here?" he asked when he spotted the two of us sitting on a stone bench. "You're lucky. People like the two of you are really lucky to be out strolling in the park."

"Sit over here," Langhua called to him.

I slid over to make room, but he didn't sit down. He stood there, absent-mindedly moving the gravel around with the sole of his shoe and picking leaves off of the tree beside him. He looked more forlorn than he had a few days earlier—something was wrong.

"Been busy? Do you have a lot of manuscripts?"

"Busy with what? All day long I've only got the same few things to do. Once I've sent off the manuscripts, my work's finished. I don't even get to see the galleys. Busy with what? Busy daydreaming, that's what!"

"Daydreaming?—gotten a letter recently?" Langhua asked him.

"A letter?—the whole thing bores me. For a man with no guts, love is a kind of punishment."

We tried to get him to sit down, but he preferred to stand. He was the kind who sat down only when no one made any room for him. He bent over and pulled up some stalks of grass at his feet. His entire face seemed masked by a gray pall.

"If you're going to fall in love, go all the way! Why make it a kind of punishment?" Langhua asked with a shake of his head.

He pulled a tiny envelope—so tiny it looked as if it might be clouded in mystery—out of his pocket. Holding it as though it were a butterfly or some other flying insect, he made as if to hand it to Langhua. But he cocked his head, indicating a change of heart, and stuffed the envelope back into his pocket.

"Is love bitter or sweet? I never loved her, did I? I didn't sleep all night the day I received that letter from home telling me that my mother had died. But I was back on my feet by the next day. So why does she— why do thoughts of her torment me day and night? No more than two weeks after we started writing to each other, I could see that I was starting to lose my hair and I had more whiskers on my face than before."

Just as we had gotten to our feet and were preparing to leave the park, another friend of ours walked up. "I'm troubled, so troubled!" It was almost a refrain.

Langhua and I stepped up onto the wooden overpass. As we turned to look back, the silhouettes of the people standing among the trees seemed to be saying to the friend who had just arrived, "I'm troubled, so troubled!"

The first thing I read in the newspaper every morning was the literary supplement. On this particular day, I noted an editorial:

> When I see lipstick on modern women, it reminds me of "blood." How do young ladies of the capitalist classes survive? Don't they survive by drinking blood? This is a clear and undeniable sign. Any mouth on which human blood has been smeared is a foul mouth. A mouth with a smell and color of blood is a sign of foulness.

I had a lot of respect for the writer. He didn't pull any punches. I continued reading the paper as I walked out into the courtyard to warm myself in the morning sun. Wang Lin was also reading the paper.

"Wang Lin, you're up early!"

"Look, look at this paragraph! What does he mean with his 'young ladies' and his 'blood'? Who does he think he's calling names!"

That day Langhua brought his editor friend home with him; he also brought some wine and some food. Langhua told me that his friend's girlfriend had gone away to college. So we drank. I drank to keep them company. Langhua drank to console his friend. As for the friend who was being consoled, he tried singing snatches of opera, but he was a terrible singer.

Our window was directly opposite Wang Lin's. Sounds from a two-stringed *huqin* floated across—Wang Lin was playing her *huqin*.

90

The weather turned hot. Wang Lin stood outside at the bench in front of her window, washing clothes before the sun climbed directly overhead.

Langhua was out when our editor friend dropped by. He paced back and forth in the courtyard, but Langhua still didn't return.

"Aren't you hot out here washing your own clothes?"

"If I wash them myself, they get clean," Wang Lin answered him, holding a bar of soap in her hand.

Langhua still hadn't returned by the time the man left.

27

Summer Night

WANG LIN sat in the courtyard for a very long time. The puppy slept fitfully at her feet.

"How're you doing? My arms are sore."

"Not so loud. My mom'll hear you."

I looked up and saw her mother standing behind the gauze window curtain. We changed the subject. She hadn't told her mother that we had rowed a boat across the Sungari River to Sun Island to have a swim.

She went back with us to swim the next day. The three of us rented a little boat, which we rowed out to the middle of the river. The air was cool and had the smell of river water. Langhua and I began to sing. Wang Lin had a higher voice than either of us. Our little boat floated on the water as though it were about to fly away.

That night we were back in the courtyard, cooling off in the night air. My arms ached from all that rowing, and my face felt puffy. The things they were talking about no longer interested me: all about falling in love, about so-and-so's fiancé, a certain schoolmate who had gotten married, dancing. I didn't listen to any of it; all I wanted to do was sleep.

"You two go ahead and talk. Me, I have to get some sleep." I said goodnight to her and to Langhua.

I accidentally stepped on the puppy as it slept at my feet. With the sound of its whimpering still in my ears, I closed the door behind me.

When the days were at their hottest, we went out to swim almost daily, so every night I went to bed early, leaving Langhua and Wang Lin alone in the darkened courtyard.

The sight of our bed made me forget everything else—Wang Lin's red lips, her young lady's melancholic ways. During all those nights I never knew exactly when Langhua came to bed. That's how those several days passed, without my knowing a thing.

"She's trying to get cozy with me. I'll tell you—those young ladies!"

"Who?"

"You mean you don't know?"

"I don't know anything." But I knew.

An impoverished tutor. Would a beautiful wealthy woman really try to get cozy with him?

"I told her straight out that we couldn't fall in love: first because of you, and second because we're so different—try to calm down a little," he told me.

We went out to row on the river again. That day there were three more people in our party. Including Wang Lin, we numbered six altogether: Chen Cheng and his woman, Langhua and me, Wang Lin and our editor friend.

The boats tied up at the riverbank bobbed on the water like so many fallen leaves. Four of us jumped into one of the boats. Naturally we left Wang Lin and our overweight friend standing alone on the rocky riverbank. It had been a little tense at first, since we were paired, but we wanted to see how the two of them would hit it off. Our boat drifted far away from the riverbank.

"You're all no good!" Wang Lin shouted over and over. "You're all no good!"

Why was she saying we were no good? Wasn't he her favorite sailor? Wouldn't he be perfectly willing to man the oars for her? Maybe it was because she saw me as her best friend and wanted to be in the same boat with me. We had drifted so far that we could no longer hear any sounds coming from the riverbank. Soon we could no longer make out the shapes of our friends standing there.

The sounds of the river, of the waves. Langhua and Chen Cheng blending their singing voices with the other sounds. Parasols held by women near and far. All these boats, these happy boats! The river was filled with happy boats; the river was filled with happiness! And the world on shore—a world free from evil!

We could no longer hear Wang Lin. Their boat had gotten underway, but a great distance still separated us.

Langhua slapped the water with his oar so that the water splashed in my face. We were moving more and more slowly, even though Langhua and Chen Cheng were sweating. The oars struck a sandbar below the water—our little boat was about to be grounded. Our two brave oarsmen jumped into the water, a couple of big fish, and pulled the boat along.

Once we had entered the cove we could moor the boat anywhere we wanted.

I had my own special way of swimming: I would propel myself along, head out of the water, so that while I seemed to be swimming, I was actually moving ahead by pushing off the bottom, sort of like an alligator, which keeps itself afloat while pushing along with all four legs.

We heard Wang Lin's shouts as her boat drew near. She hurriedly took off her outer clothing and, like me, began propelling herself through the water by pushing off the bottom. She was very happy, moving through the water with considerable enthusiasm.

As we all played on the sandbar, she became quite chummy, much to our surprise. She opened her parasol to shield the man who was sharing her boat from the sun's rays; she was protecting him. Chen Cheng tossed some sand at him. "Ling, heads up!"

Wang Lin and Ling lined up and returned the fire with sand.

Even after our boat had left the cove and was out on the river again, the two of them were still walking on the sandbar.

"You go on ahead," Wang Lin said, "and we'll see who gets to the riverbank first."

The heat of the sun's rays on the surface of the water began to lessen. Our boat drifted along with the river's current, but we saw no trace of theirs. Several other boats passed us, several parasols went by, but not Wang Lin's. The winds over the river picked up as the sun set in the west; the waves were higher. We were beginning to worry about their boat, which Li called our "lost ship."

The four of us stood on the riverbank, waiting for the "lost ship." It never occurred to us that they would take the long way around. They arrived from upstream.

Wang Lin had stopped saying that we were no good. Her hair was blowing in the wind, and she was as excited as could be. She seemed to have had much more enjoyment out of this river excursion than the rest of us, a lot more.

I was surprised to note in the newspaper the following morning that the editor had written a poem. The meaning was more or less as follows: I wouldn't mind if the boat capsized, for I'd happily sink to the bottom with that beautiful girl.

Unfortunately, the way I say it erases all the poetic feeling. Anyway, it was altogether different from his comments over the previous days, remarks such as: modern girls survive by drinking "blood," young ladies' mouths are smeared with "blood," and so on. Things had changed. And this new line of his was far more refined than the old one. He was now saying that modern girls were goddesses, whereas he had said earlier that they were demons.

Wang Lin and Langhua didn't have so much to talk about in the evenings any longer. Now she came over only when Ling, the editor, dropped by. But Ling came over to our place more and more frequently.

"Let's go out a little earlier tonight—we'll have more time to have fun. Wait for me out on the street." Wang Lin didn't say such things anymore. There was no longer any need for her to go to Sun Island with us.

Ling took walks with this girl who "drank human blood." When they went to the movies, he was no longer afraid that she would drink his blood. Afraid? Why, he often kissed those red lips, feeling that her mouth was attractive precisely *because* it was as red as blood.

Calling young ladies demons had stemmed from envy; it was his way of reaching out to grab her, for he was afraid that she would get away.

As they walked along, Wang Lin's high-heeled shoes and Ling's patent-leather shoes tapped the sidewalk in perfect unison.

28

The Tutor Is a Criminal

A PERSON'S silhouette flashed past our window; then came two raps on our window pane. It was Wang Lin's father.

What did he want? Langhua had been gone for a long time—over half an hour!

I opened the door. I must have looked still half asleep as I walked outside rubbing my eyes. Wang Lin's older sister, the one with the frighteningly pale face, was sitting on the steps in front of her door. Lin Qin (the dog) was running back and forth in the courtyard, making the pale-faced girl sitting on the steps very angry. She yelled at the dog to stop just as Wang Lin walked outside, smoke rising from the cigarette in her mouth. Wang Lin joined her sister on the steps without even waving to me. Their maid Xiao Ju was walking in the courtyard on her very best behavior.

I stood beneath their living-room window listening to Langhua talking inside. I couldn't see him or the people he was talking to, because the gauze window curtain completely blocked my view of the room. I stood there without moving a muscle—was it a Japanese! What was going on? But no Japanese spoke, and I wasn't about to go over and ask the girls, who were sitting there with frowns on their faces.

Were we being terrorized over the printing of our book? Had the Japanese found out about that book of ours, the one we hadn't submitted for inspection?

"They received an anonymous letter, warning that Wang Yuxiang's teacher was planning to kidnap him."

I nodded my head and walked back to the spot beneath the window, but now I couldn't make out what was being said inside.

"Third Mistress, dinner's ready!" Xiao Ju called her in for dinner, casting a cautious glance at me at the same time.

Over the next three or four days, Wang Yuxiang, who was being watched over carefully by his elder sisters, didn't dare go out to the compound gate.

The tutor really did look a little like a criminal, and who would be willing to guarantee that he wasn't? He never wore a necktie, and he had only one jacket—a lined jacket, which he wore during the winter, the fall, and the spring.

For two weeks or more, Wang Yuxiang didn't so much as come over to our window; the adults in his family had obviously warned him, "Your teacher isn't someone we know that much about."

29

The Book

THE light from the constantly flickering candle hurt my eyes. Copy, copy.

"How many words?"

"Just over three thousand."

"Your hand must be tired. Why don't you take a break? You don't want to ruin your eyes." Langhua stretched and went over to lie down on the bed. He put his hands behind his head, resting his back against the metal frame of the bed. I kept writing, the nib of my pen making scratching noises on the paper.

I could hear the dog barking through the gauze window curtain. Then I heard footsteps. Someone was coming toward us from the direction of the main gate. An uncontrollable terror struck my heart.

"Who's coming? Go out and take a look."

Langhua opened the door; Li and Chen Cheng walked in. They were comrades from the drama troupe, so they must have brought some scripts over. Rather than go over and get some for myself, I just let them take a seat on the edge of the bed.

"Yin sure is busy. What's she writing now?"

"Nothing. I'm doing some copying." I picked up the pen and started in again.

Snatches of their conversation began to break my concentration. I was writing more and more incorrect characters, or omitting characters, or duplicating them.

Mosquitoes were biting my legs. When they began to gather under the lamp, I laid down my pen and stopped writing.

Help! The room was swarming with mosquitoes. The front door was wide open! A stray puppy wandered in, turned around, and ran back outside with his tail between his legs. We closed the door, but the mosquitoes continued flying around the room—I scratched my itching ear, my legs, my feet—my knuckles were all swollen, and my hand became so sore from scratching mosquito bites that I had to stop. My lips were badly swollen, and the skin around my eyes felt hot and tight. I kept scratching myself all over until I felt that I didn't have enough hands to do the job right.

"How's the book coming?" Smoke curled from the cigarette in Li's mouth.

"Only one story to go," Langhua answered him.

"What's the cover going to look like?"

"That's what we're waiting on."

I went along with him to the printers' the next day, a trip that brought me great pleasure. Nearly completed copies of the book were neatly stacked; the sight evoked feelings of happiness exceeding those from my childhood when Mother had finished making me a new dress. I walked up to one of the typesetters. He was just then setting one of the titles with large, square pieces of lead type. A surge of emotion overcame me as I recognized one of my stories: "Night Winds."

That day we splurged on some piroshki. Langhua said he wanted to celebrate the printing of the book. I went over to the counter and ordered two glasses of vodka, telling the man that we were drinking to celebrate the printing of our book.

Spurred on by our expansive mood, we turned into a couple of kids! We walked over to the park, where we sat down under a big tree and cooled off, feeling that the park was the perfect place to be. We looked up through the branches of the tree at the sky. Some Russian children were playing in the dirt. Not many people were in the park, since it wasn't even noon yet. Some Japanese women were strolling under parasols. The ice-cream vendor was washing out some cups in his stall. I suddenly felt thirsty, but we weren't attracted by the row upon row of soft drinks in transparent bottles. I hadn't acquired the habit of drinking that stuff—in all my time in the park I'd never bought a single bottle.

"Let's go home and have a glass of water." Drinking cool water at home was the answer—it was free.

I opened the door and took off my wide-brimmed straw hat as I entered the room. As soon as I had my fill of water, I suggested putting our hats back on and taking a stroll along the riverbank.

So we headed toward the river, Langhua barefoot and wearing a pair of shorts, me wearing a short skirt.

We looked like a couple of fishermen. We stopped from time to time to see ourselves reflected in windows along the street.

"Let's go rowing. It's such a nice day!" I urged as soon as we had reached the riverbank.

"We only have twenty cents left—but we can do it if you'd like. Let's splurge a little!"

We climbed into a double-oared boat. A straw mat

was spread over the bottom. We told the boatman we'd pay fifteen cents for one hour. We weren't planning on taking a swim, since we hadn't even brought our swimsuits with us. The boatman pushed us away from the bank, and we rowed out to the middle of the river. We plied the oars, heading downriver with the current, as the riverbank receded. We came to a little island completely by accident, a sandbar that jutted out in the middle of the river. Langhua jumped boldly up onto the sandbar. I hesitated timidly, fearing that the little island might sink back into the river at any moment.

We had a swim after all, removing our clothes there on the little island. Langhua stripped to the skin at once, but I looked over at the people washing clothes by the edge of the river. Even though I couldn't see their faces, I put the boat between them and me, slipped into the river, then took off my clothes under the water. I stayed as close to the sandbar as possible, so that the current wouldn't carry me away.

Waves lapped at the bottom of the boat as I held onto the side, my head above water, the rest of me submerged. The light reflecting off the surface of the water and the sun's rays shining down on me seemed to remove me from the world of mortals. As I lay on the sandbar basking in the sun, a small rowboat came out of the north in our direction. This threw me into a panic, since I had no time to get dressed. *What'll I do? Into the water!* After the boat passed by, I climbed back onto the sandbar.

I put on my clothes. Langhua was still naked. He was looking for his shirt, which he said he had hung over the side of the boat to dry after washing it. But it was gone. Then he spotted a white object floating on the surface some distance away. He was sure it was his shirt. So we got into the boat and rowed toward the white object, which was drifting slowly in the water. It was a fish, a dead, white fish.

We weren't all that upset over the loss of his shirt. Laughing and shouting at the top of his lungs, Langhua scooped the fish out of the water with his bare hands, convinced that it took skill to scoop a fish right out of the river that way.

"This will be our dinner. You can fry it up."

"We can't eat a dead fish. It's probably spoiled."

He quickly spread the fish's gills to show me. "Look. Look here. How can something as red as that be spoiled?"

He didn't quiet down until we had reached the river-bank.

"What'll I do? I can't walk down Central Avenue without a shirt on, can I?" He had calmed down completely by then and had probably forgotten all about the fish.

I ran home to get him a shirt. By the time I got back I was bathed in sweat, but he was just sitting there at the edge of the river drinking tea with some stevedores. The air underneath the canvas awning was cooled by gusts of wind blowing off the river.

I expected him to ask me, "Aren't you hot?" But his first concern was over our dinner, not me. "Where'd you put the fish? Have you washed it off in cold water?"

"Give me five cents to buy some vinegar. I'll need vinegar if I'm going to fry the fish."

"I don't have a penny left. I bought some tea. Can't you see that?"

Carried away by our happiness, we had spent all our money and had lost a shirt in the river, all in return for a dead fish.

Just before we started eating the fish, Langhua said, "To celebrate the printing of our book, I'm treating you to this fish dinner!"

We had entered our creative-writing phase, our first phase, launched by the printing of this book.

On the fourteenth day of the eighth lunar month, the eve of the Autumn Festival, we went to the printers' to bind our books with staples. We spent the entire day binding copies. Afterward, Langhua kneaded his back with his fists; I had a sore back too.

Langhua went out and hired a little pushcart, onto which we loaded a hundred copies of the book. Just as night was falling, we started the walk home, the bell around the horse's neck loudly leading the way.

Copies of the book covered our floor. All of our friends were holding copies of the book. All we talked about was the book.

Rumors about the book began immediately: confiscation—Japanese MPs were out to make arrests!

No arrests were made, but the books were confiscated. Within a very few days, books sent to the bookshops were taken off the shelves.

30

The Drama Troupe

THE book brought terror. As night fell we walked out of the People's Education Hall with the other members of the drama troupe, having completed our rehearsal of the play. The atmosphere of terror made me uneasy about my own home. The streetlamps came on just as we entered the courtyard, the other people following on our heels. The door and the window were both securely closed, as always, which removed one anxiety. I could be confident that no evil had as yet been in our home.

Disappointment. Langhua had the key to the door. We would have to wait for him. Everyone sat down by the stairs under the window and began eating the melons that Li had bought.

Wang Lin was smoking her customary cigarette as she smiled at us from behind the parted gauze curtain in her window. Chen Cheng raised up one of the melons in his hand.

"No, thanks," she said through the window, shaking her head.

I was totally preoccupied. A nagging concern continued to occupy my thoughts even after they had finished talking about that night's rehearsal. Why couldn't they leave soon so that I could take care of the trunk! It was as though Langhua and I were going to be incriminated by something in that trunk.

They left, and Langhua pulled the trunk out from under the bed. After placing a candle on the floor, we began to take care of the contents. Books and papers were strewn all over the floor, but we found nothing incriminating among them. That didn't instill much confidence in us, however. We were afraid that a page in one of the books might have an abusive reference to "Manchukuo" or something else, so we leafed carefully through each and every book. When we had finished, nothing was left in the trunk. We had even burned a photograph of Gorki, the flames temporarily singeing our faces. I was throwing things into the fire as fast as I could, as though the Japanese MPs were on their way to arrest us at that very moment.

As we sat there drinking tea, we knew we had done what we must. We had no more worries. I was absent-mindedly turning a piece of blotting paper over and over as I sat there with my back straight, feeling quite composed. My heart was as relaxed as a bowstring that has been pulled taut then released. I glanced at what had been written on the blotting paper with red pencil—uh oh! Those words could get us into real trouble! "Japs, running dogs, God-damned 'Manchukuo' . . ."

Without even taking another look, I tossed the paper into the fire.

"Hey! That was perfectly good blotting paper! Langhua reacted with a forlorn stomp of his foot. When he realized that it was already starting to burn, he railed, "How could you burn a big piece of blotting paper like that? The fire's made you giddy. After you've burned everything, what will you use?"

He was showing far too much concern over that piece of blotting paper. His distress was beginning to get to me. What was more important? Blotting paper or our personal safety?

"You'd consign a jacket to the flames just to get rid of a louse!" Langhua complained. "Couldn't you have just cut off the part where the words were written?"

Who had time to think of that? What a fool I'd been! Like someone who throws away an apple because of a bruise!

We put our postcards commemorating the founding of "Manchukuo" on the table; they'd been given to us by a friend, a thick bundle of them. We also put out two books with the word "Manchukuo" on the covers. We had no idea what the books were about, simply putting them on the table without even opening them. The table had once looked quite impressive, with copies of the epic poem "On Encountering Sorrow," *The Lyrics of Li Houzhu*, and other literary works. There had also been a copy of *Mathematics*, the textbook Langhua had used as a tutor. These, and a book entitled *World Revolutionary History* all had to go. According to Langhua, the last title included mention of Japanese oppression in Korea, so it couldn't stay on the table. As soon as I learned the significance of that particular book, I made up my mind to throw it into the fire at once. I leaped to my feet, but Langhua caught me in time. "Are you crazy? Have you lost your mind?"

I didn't say another word. Even after we had turned out the lamp, I barely dared to breathe. As I lay there in the dark my eyes were wide open. The dog out in the courtyard was barking more loudly, the door hinges squeaked. For me, everything that could make a sound was noisier that night than usual, and things that normally were silent had found their voices. The ceiling was making noise, the tiles on the roof of the Western-style houses were whistling in the wind—whistling, whistling.

Langhua placed his hand on my chest—my stifled chest. The metal gate rattled, startling me.

"Don't be frightened. What do we have? Nothing! The rumors aren't true. Damn it! We won't worry unless we get arrested. Now go to sleep. If you don't get enough sleep, you'll have a headache tomorrow."

He pressed down gently on my chest, as with a child frightened by a nightmare, whose heart is beating wildly under its mother's hand.

One day our troupe went to a movie theater to rehearse a play. We left my place in small groups. When we formed up ranks again, we discovered that one of our number, Xu Zhi, was missing. He had never missed a rehearsal before; he had always shown up without fail, so everyone thought he must be ill.

It was a large stage with a lovely curtain. I was playing the role of an old woman who was supposed to cry out and become ill. We arranged four chairs to form a bed so that I could practice collapsing onto it. But all I managed to do was bump my hip painfully.

The first scene we rehearsed for the theater owner was from *The Thief*, with Langhua, playing the role of James, talking to the wife of his lawyer, played by Li. Since I was acting in one of the other plays, my turn hadn't come by the time we left the theater.

Owing to some unacceptable conditions, we couldn't put on our public performance. We kept waiting for our chance, all the while growing more and more suspicious. Weren't we going to be allowed to perform?

We had taken three months to prepare three plays. It would be a shame if we couldn't perform them before an audience.

"Any news on your book?"

"No. We can't live our lives in fear of wolves or tigers. In times like these, we have to go ahead and take what comes." Langhua was standing firm.

31

Pale Faces

THE hand of terror pressed down on our drama troupe. Chen Cheng's pale face appeared even paler in the moonlight. The paleness of his face reminded us of the seriousness of the situation. His shoes made scraping sounds as he walked down the cobbled street, which had been bathed by autumn rains. As he, Li, Langhua, and I walked down a long street, Li said, "Remember the other day at rehearsal, when Xu Zhi didn't show up? He's been under arrest for a week! We didn't even know."

"Don't say any more. You shouldn't talk about such things when we're outside." I nudged his shoulder.

We walked along furtively, Langhua and Chen Cheng in one row, Li and I in another. Whenever someone walked up behind me, I made a careful note of his presence before he had a chance to note mine. We felt as though everyone knew what we were doing. The streetlights were a different color, although we barely noticed the lights as we walked ahead nervously.

Li and Chen Cheng had dropped by to inform us that Old Bo, a member of our drama troupe, hadn't dared to go home for three days in a row because a secret agent was stationed outside his door. He was getting ready to flee.

We went over to visit our overweight friend and see if he had any ideas as to what we should do. "Since the affairs of the X X Department are top secret, I don't know a thing about this matter. I haven't heard a word." He paced the floor.

We returned home, locked the door behind us, and dug back into the trunk. We knew nothing was left to be taken out, but we rummaged through it anyway. Then we took the copies of our book from the entryway out to the woodshed. The sight of our book no longer brought us any pleasure—it had become a curse!

Lao Qin's face had also turned pale. We noticed this the following day when we met him on the street. We didn't say a word, because Langhua had already confided to him what was going on.

There was nothing we could do except flee. But with no money, where could we go? Troubling times were once again upon us. Such times originally had been caused by hunger. We had no sooner solved the problem of food than our days had suddenly become filled reality of an evil totally alien to us. Who had the Japanese MPs arrested the night before last? Who had Japanese MPs arrested the night before last? Who had they arrested last night? We heard that the person arrested yesterday had once been affiliated with our drama troupe.

Our ears were filled with these things, making us uneasy whenever we went out. Then, as we were walking along Central Avenue, it suddenly happened: someone grabbed Langhua by the shoulder—a tall, thin man—

and started leading him away. He turned at the intersection, Langhua following close behind him. Not a word was exchanged. He seemed to be in a daze as he left my side and walked off with the man. At first my line of vision was blocked by a crowd of people in front of the movie theater, but Langhua and the man appeared to be on such close terms that my heart barely skipped a beat. They started walking back my way, shoulder to shoulder, not a trace of emotion on either of their faces. Then they turned and walked back—this time they kept walking, without turning to head back my way. *What sort of strategy is this? Are they leading him into a trap?*

But the man wasn't there to arrest him, after all. He was a friend, a very ridiculous friend! It had all happened so suddenly! A person whose nerves are on edge could have a nervous breakdown. "Watch out! There's danger! Two members of your drama troupe have been arrested." He acted very strangely there on the street, saying over and over to us, "You'll have to make preparations, you'll have to!"

"Preparations for what? It won't do any good. I'll take what comes," Langhua said to him, without so much as shrugging his shoulders.

So many things were happening these days. Our editor friend, Ling, had run off. Wang Lin's pale face appeared in our courtyard—she had been drinking. She said she had been drunk all night long. She told us how Ling had seen her to the door the night before, how he had asked for her little paring knife—she was reliving it as she talked. Her face was very pale, as though everything bad had happened all at once.

Our friends began to change. Wang Lin, who did little but walk back and forth in the courtyard, had changed.

Xu Zhi was the only member of the drama troupe we actually had lost, but with the reign of terror in progress, no one mentioned the drama troupe again.

32

Winter Again

THE snow falling beyond the window was like white velvet. It fell continually, all day long. My frostbitten feet from the year before had healed completely. This year they would not be frozen. The fire in the stove roared, occasionally crackling as sparks flew from one of the pieces of kindling. The window never had a chance to frost up. The firewood wasn't stacked in front of the window this year but filled the woodshed out back.

We had made up our minds to leave "Manchukuo" and be a part of our own country again. Whenever we went to the bookstore, there wasn't a magazine to be found. The only books for sale were old faded ones that three years earlier had been displayed in the front window.

We had to leave, we just had to leave.

We asked every friend we ran into, "Which month is the ocean most calm? What's it like aboard an ocean-going ship?" We had never been to sea, and the ocean-going ships were so enormous that the mere sight of one in a picture book filled us with dread. So we stopped in front of the window of the International Travel Agency every time we passed it, pausing at length to gaze at the large poster that stood inside.

We tried to guess the height of the actual ship. We were told that during calm seas the waves were three feet high, so as I stood in front of the window, I tried gauging with my hand how many times higher than the waves the ship was. The difference was staggering! It was at least twenty times higher than the waves. That meant the ship was sixty feet high!

"How can it be sixty feet?" Langhua challenged me.

He tried it himself. "You see! The waves are about—they're three feet, so the ship is twenty-three feet high."

Sometimes I would repeat over and over, "Is it that high? It can't be! But then again it *might* be!" Langhua would lose his temper, and we would nearly get into an argument right there on the street over the height of the ship.

Our friends didn't know that we were preparing to leave. One day at our overweight friend's home, as we were raising our wine glasses to salute the roast chicken, Langhua nearly let the news slip out. I cautioned him not to say anything, but it eventually got said anyway.

"You're better off leaving! You should have left a long time ago!" Our overweight friend had often said, "Langhua, you really ought to leave. I can give you some travel money. Every day I go to the X X Bureau, where I hear them trying cases. That whip of theirs really sets up a racket! Ai! Leave! What would it be like if one of my friends wound up there? How could I stand to listen to the sound of that whip! Every time I see those people, I think of you."

Lao Qin dropped by, wearing a brand new overcoat; his hat looked new also. Before anyone even had a chance to comment, he said, "Have you all noticed that I'm wearing a new overcoat? I have to get to Shanghai. I've been running around having some new clothes made in case I need something to pawn after I get there. New clothes can bring a higher price in one of the second-hand shops there."

We were really glad to hear this. Langhua couldn't hold back any longer: "We're leaving too. We have to. All we're accomplishing by staying here is giving them a chance to flay the skin off our bones!" When he finished, he laughed. "When are you leaving?" he asked.

"How about you?"

"We haven't decided for sure."

"The best time to leave is in May or June, when the seas are calmer."

"Then let's go together!"

Lao Qin didn't believe that we were leveling with him. Everyone else began discussing the subject of leaving, trying to come up with the best way to go about it. They were afraid we'd be stopped on the road, stopped and questioned. We had no friends in Shanghai and no money. The conversation was exhilarating: true-to-life yet almost like a dream. Lao Qin had been to Shanghai before. He told us what Foochow Road was like, what it was like to be poor in Shanghai.

It was snowing when he left, so I added a piece of wood to the fire. By then it was time to make dinner. I thought about last year and about this year. I looked down at my hands—my knuckles were a little swollen, but I was just as tall as I had been then, and just as skinny.

I knew this house of ours like the back of my hand, so well that I could even point out where there were extra nails on the wall and in the ceiling.

And Langhua? He had neither gained nor lost weight. He was the same as he had always been since the day I had met him: high cheekbones, small eyes, a large mouth, and a straight nose.

"What'll we eat? Noodles or rice?"

Surprisingly, we had both. Quite the opposite from the year before. I was suddenly overcome with thoughts of the past—managing to borrow twenty cents, or perhaps only ten—he'd return empty-handed—taking my new padded jacket to the pawnshop.

As I thought of my frostbitten feet, instinctively I looked down at them, then had thoughts of firewood. I had so much of it now. *Burn it!* I went out and brought some in.

"Close the door! It's freezing!" Langhua screamed.

He paced the floor, his hands stuffed into his pockets, which is what he did any time the subject of leaving arose; he often paced for as long as half an hour.

Since autumn we had had an electric lamp installed, under the light of which I copied over some of my manuscripts. He was out having a good time. This, too, was different from the year before; this year he no longer went out as a tutor.

33

A Black Shape in Front of the Gate

SINCE the night before, we had become more frightened than ever by the rattling of the metal gate. Every time we heard the sound, we rushed out into the entryway to take a look. At least four or five times. But it was never what we expected. We were hoping it wouldn't be.

Early in the morning, one of Langhua's friends, a student at a certain school, came into our room and, without removing his school cap or taking a seat, said, "The reports are pretty bad, the ones I hear about you, that is. They got one of my fellow students."

"When?"

"Yesterday. We'd just begun winter vacation, and he was planning to return home. Early this morning the Japanese MPs came and searched our dormitory with a fine-toothed comb. They turned over every single mattress and found a copy of *War and Peace*."

"So what?"

"You're going to have to be more careful. I've heard that someone is out to get you."

"I'm not known as being anti-'Manchukuo' or anti-Japanese, so what's there to be afraid of?"

"Don't talk like that. They take people without any pretext at all. Just think, they confiscated a copy of *War and Peace* as some kind of evidence. Although I can't imagine what they expect to find in *that!*"

He left, but not before we had asked him who was out to get us. He wouldn't say. Someone else dropped by after a while—he was just as nervous as the first man, but during those days everyone's nerves were on edge.

"You two had better go into hiding. Things are looking bad! Out on the street they're saying that there was something fishy about the drama troupe, that its members were up to no good. How about the one they arrested—have they released him yet?"

After we saw him out, we went over to take a walk on the frozen pond at the park. Children were ice-skating when we arrived—Japanese children, Russian children, Chinese children.

We made a turn around the frozen pond, feeling generally uneasy—we didn't talk to each other. A heavy mood was upon us.

"Let's have noodles tonight!" he said when he spotted the noodle stand north of the road. I went over and bought some raw noodles.

After we returned home, we couldn't read, we couldn't study our Russian, so we started preparing dinner. But even that didn't lighten our mood, as though we really didn't want to eat anything at all.

Our salt jar, sitting on the shelf, was filled with pure white salt; alongside it was a jar filled with dried shrimps, a soy-sauce bottle, a bottle of vinegar, one of sesame oil, and another one filled with a meat paste. A sack of rice rested in the corner alongside a sack of noodles, and the woodshed was stacked to the ceiling—but these things weren't enough to satisfy us. We had found more pleasure in eating rice with a pinch of salt the year before than in eating the noodles with meat paste now.

I spotted the silhouette of a man from the Market Street intersection. There was something different about this one—he looked like a Japanese MP. I kept walking, concerned that Langhua would be frightened if he knew what I had seen.

I took another eight or ten steps, but I couldn't go on. The man, who was wearing high-topped boots, was pacing back and forth in front of the metal gate. I stopped to take a closer look. Langhua had also spotted him right off. We felt like running away. The man was waiting at the entrance for us! There was no reason to doubt it. An "iron donkey" was waiting on the southern side of the street, toward which the Japanese was now heading. It seemed obvious from his manner that he was trying to pick up whatever bits of conversation he could.

To hell with home. It was time to flee! But where?

The Japanese wasn't wearing a sword at his side or, for that matter, any other weapons. There was even some doubt in our minds that he was actually out to arrest anyone. We walked into a shop on the southern side of the street where things like bread and vodka were sold. We bought a loaf of bread. I had said nothing about sausage, but the shopkeeper cut a piece off for us; I was too busy looking out the window to pay any attention. The swordless Japanese turned and walked off slowly.

What a joke it had all been—we had spent thirty-five cents in the shop; we walked out through the glass door carrying thirty-five cents' worth of bread and sausage. But even if it had been more money than that, and we had just thrown it into the street, it wouldn't have mattered.

"What did we go and buy this for? Now I won't be able to buy any socks tomorrow!" The danger had passed. There was a tone of frustration in my voice as I answered, "I don't know. Who told you to buy it? Who're you trying to blame?"

Langhua, who was walking ahead of me, opened the door with a loud shove. We were met by a blast of hot air.

34

The Decision

WE had to leave. Even though things had cooled down a bit, we were determined to leave. But when?

May!

Five months to go. We were constantly making calculations under the light of the lamp: how much money we should borrow from so-and-so, so-and-so would be good for half of our travel expenses . . .

The mere thought of leaving filled us with excitement, but it also brought a sense of sadness. That's why my hand trembled as I poured tea.

"Let's be wanderers! Harbin isn't our home, anyway, so let's just be wanderers!" Langhua raised his tea glass in salute, but he put it back down without taking a drink.

Tears filled my eyes.

"Why are you so sad? Let's just go. As long as I'm by your side, you don't have to be afraid, no matter where we go. What are you so sad about? Lao Qiao, don't be so sad."

I hung my head as I said, "What'll we do with our utensils?"

"You're acting like a child! What's the big deal about a few utensils!"

I laughed to myself; I laughed *at* myself. I made a turn around the room, but I couldn't shake the sorrow in my heart, so I hung my head again.

Hadn't Comrade Xu from the drama troupe been released? And hadn't he reported that they'd forced cold water down his throat? I thought of this, thought of what it must be like for someone to be taken in, nearly drowned with cold water, and beaten with a rubber hose until he was no longer a person. Let's leave. We had to leave!

35

A Young Woman from the South

LANGHUA brought some news home with him; the first thing he said to me when he returned from his driving lesson was, "I've made a new friend, someone from Shanghai, a student in middle school. She's going to drop by in a couple of days."

Two days later there was a knock on the door. The first thing I noticed was the lovely red band tied around her hair. She said she had come to see me. Lao Wang had brought her over, and everyone began to chat right away; everyone, it seemed, but me—I just listened to the others.

"I've only been here forty days, so my Mandarin's still pretty bad, but I can understand most of what you're saying. I only met Lao Wang after I got here. It was interesting the way things worked out. I was reading a polemic on drama in the newspaper one day, and I found myself sympathizing with the author, a certain Langhua. So I asked some friends who this Mr. Langhua was. I thought the piece was really well written. So Lao Wang introduced me to Langhua."

I just nodded my head, since I wasn't in the habit of saying much to strangers. She crossed over and picked up a newspaper from the table, searching for the latest installment of the polemic. I looked her over very slowly; she was probably doing the same to me. She was beautiful, plain and neat—no lipstick, no perm— and the red satin band in her hair increased the appearance of charm. She was beautiful and fresh. Her pale grape-colored gown was decorated with yellow flowers, and this was the only thing about her that I found less than beautiful. But even that detracted only slightly from her loveliness. She had been invited to stay for dinner with us that night, but before the meal was served, Wang Lin dropped by. She had come over to ask Langhua to go ice-skating with her.

"Isn't Langhua home?" she asked through the slightly opened window. This was followed by an "Oh!"

"What are you doing here?" Wang Lin came inside.

"Is there any law against my being here?"

I was surprised that they apparently knew each other so well.

"How do you two know each other?"

"We met at a dance hall," she told me after Wang Lin had left.

I deduced from this comment that Miss Cheng often went to dance halls. Wang Lin was a lovely young lady; so, of course, was Miss Cheng. From that point on, I paid no more attention to Miss Cheng.

I have little interest in making friends with people whose environments differ from mine.

Langhua returned with his ice skates slung over his shoulder. Wang Lin must have spotted him in the courtyard, for she followed him in. The activity level in the room rose dramatically. Wang Lin ran home to fetch her *huqin* and her harmonica. Langhua started singing "Yang Tinghui Seated in the Palace Garden."

"Hey, hey! What're you singing that for? That's for someone with the 'heart of a slave'!" Wang Lin teased him.

The war of words in the newspaper had been fought over classic opera, and Langhua had pointedly written that the singing of classic opera was for people with "the hearts of slaves."

Wang Lin shrugged her shoulders and laughed, pressing her back against the warm wall; the heat promptly turned her face red. That, plus her red lips, her permed hairdo, and her green velvet dress, gave her an appearance quite the opposite of Miss Cheng's. She had the airs of a Western young lady, while Miss Cheng was very dark, a very dark young lady.

A few days later, Langhua went out and borrowed a pair of ice skates for me, so I began going along with them to the skating rink. Miss Cheng often came over to our place to borrow my ice skates. Sometimes we all went together, so naturally we got to know each other better and better. She was far more familiar with Langhua than with me, and she even wrote him letters. They saw each other regularly, yet she still wrote him letters.

Some days later, Miss Cheng came over to eat some noodles at our place, so I went out into the kitchen to prepare them.

" . . . Psst . . . psst . . ."

As soon as I walked into the room, they started talking about something else! After eating only a small bowl of noodles, Miss Cheng said, "I'm full."

I noticed that she had become darker than usual over

the past few days, as though her "worries" had increased. But it was more than worries, for worried people are seldom excited, whereas Miss Cheng showed signs of excitement.

I was too busy clearing off the table to see her to the door when she left, so Langhua saw her out.

"Do you have a letter for me?" I heard her ask at the door.

Maybe that wasn't exactly what she said, but they were definitely whispering to each other. Then Langhua said in full voice, "No."

Over the next few days, Miss Cheng seldom dropped by, probably to avoid me.

Miss Cheng was returning to the South, so she came over to say goodbye. My presence kept her from telling Langhua all about her worries, so she took those worries with her back to the South.

36

The Stranger

A VERY odd guest came to our house. At the time, I was in the kitchen frying flatcakes, since it was nearly the dinner hour. I burned half of one of the flatcakes, and some of the others actually caught fire and sent out billows of smoke. That was because I kept running into the other room to listen in on the conversation, eventually forgetting that I was supposed to be preparing dinner. The cakes placed on the table that night were so terrible that I finally had to go out and buy some bread for dinner.

They were still talking, so instead of clearing the table when dinner was finished, I just stood foolishly by the door.

They were talking about bitter experiences, although once in a while they laughed. Our guest was a representative of the Panshi People's Revolutionary Army . . . I recall only that he had a very ruddy face.

37

Spring Again

THE sun brought some warmth, the icy banks of the Sungari River receded, the melting ice merged with the river water, and the number of sleighs pulled by servants decreased. People no longer dared to drive automobiles across the river. The Sungari River had lost its winter solemnity. The snow atop the river was no longer a dazzling white but had turned gray. Before many days had passed, the ice was already flowing along with the river water. It was a beautiful sight, this river flowing with a purpose but seemingly without purpose; chunks of ice, big and small, crashed against each other as they flowed with the current—"ping, ping"—sounding like ceramic pots banging together, like pieces of glass banging together. As I stood on the riverbank I daydreamed: *Where do these chunks of ice go? To the sea? They'll probably never make it that far, for the sun's rays will surely melt them before they reach their destination.*

Still they flowed on, tranquilly, as though they were alive and far happier than we humans.

We met some friends by the river that day, with whom we agreed to take a stroll on the bridge that crossed the river. Langhua and I walked ahead of the others, the river beneath us flowing to the east. The steel rails sang in the open air above the river, chunks of ice floated in the river, white clouds filled the sky.

We walked to the end of the bridge but still had not reached the outlying area of the city. We saw no velvety green grass, no green trees. Why did it take so long for spring to reach the northern frontier? We felt like having a drink, so we walked back along the riverbank. But we never found a wineshop, for the area north of the river was like a ghetto—buildings made of mud and fences made of grass and sticks.

"Why haven't we heard any chickens?"

"Why do you want to hear them?" We were sitting on the bank, wiping our faces. It was a hot day for walking.

After that, we went over to look at a warship sunk during a 1929 battle with the Russians. We could still see its name—it was called "Great Victory." We shared our thoughts regarding the warship, but everything we said was a bunch of nonsense. Someone said that it had sunk when the boiler had burst; someone else said that it had sunk when the pilot had been killed. It was riddled with bullet holes, a useless cripple. It reminded one of a soldier who has lost a leg on the battlefield. Being maimed, he is called a cripple.

The battered warship lay there alongside the wharf, turning to rust.

38

Illness

As I was making breakfast I opened the window to let in the special air of spring, which soon filled the room. I had placed some peeled potatoes alongside the stove and continued working with the paring knife in my hand. One after another I placed the potatoes, which were pale yellow in color and spongy to the touch, on the stove. The rice gruel was bubbling in the pot alongside, and as I peeled the potatoes I thought: *Every last chunk of ice on the river has melted by now, and buds have probably already begun to appear on the elm trees in the park. It's been three days since I've been to the park, so I'll have to go over and take a look right after breakfast.*

"Langhua, what are you doing out there? You can help by getting me a bucket of water."

"That's not my job. Get it yourself!" He was out pacing the courtyard, his mind on another article he was planning to write. I was in a pretty good mood, so I went out myself. I flipped the bucket over noisily. After emerging from the Wang's kitchen, I sidled across the courtyard with my heavy load. The water in the bucket sloshed from side to side.

The vegetables were ready, the rice was ready. As soon as breakfast was over, I was going to the river, to the park. Spring was fleeting by overhead; it was passing through my heart. But I couldn't eat. Sharp pains in my stomach suddenly doubled me over.

I called Langhua inside. My shouts startled him, but the pain was quickly getting to be more than I could bear.

He went to get a doctor for me, returning with a throat specialist.

"Have you got appendicitis?" the doctor asked me.

I was in such pain. How was I supposed to know if I had appendicitis or not? My eyes turned dark, and the throat specialist gave me a shot of pain killer just beneath my shoulder.

"Doctor Zhang, we'll have to ask you to take care of your own carfare for the time being. We'll bring that and the money for the medicine over to you in a few days," Langhua said to the doctor.

We didn't have a dime to our name, so we couldn't very well ask another doctor over to give me another shot, which was too bad, since the pain was still there.

Langhua went out again, but I didn't know why. I can't describe the feelings I experienced as I waited for him to return.

A week passed, and I was still unable to sit up in bed. On the ninth day, Langhua brought some fresh flowers home with him, which he put into a vase and placed on the table.

"Are the flowers blooming?"

"Not only that, the trees have all turned green!"

The trees were green! How many different things associated with spring occurred to me then I don't know, but I felt I just had to get out of bed and see for myself. Unfortunately, I was powerless to do anything. My legs were so rubbery that I might as well not have had any legs at all—I couldn't even stand up.

My headache was a little better, so I was able to sleep soundly at night. Someone told Langhua that a medical clinic somewhere in the city had been set up for the poor, where they didn't charge for medication.

Naturally, I struggled to my feet to go over there. It was a sunny day, so I changed into some clean clothes, walked with difficulty out the gate, and got into a ricksha. Langhua walked alongside—at first he kept a hand on the ricksha, but before long he was walking by himself on the sidewalk. There weren't any sprouts on the trees that lined the streets—they had already turned into green leaves!

We entered the clinic and walked over to the registration desk, where we gave our names. It was a long room, furnished with several benches. Some of the people were already being examined. A Russian woman in a white uniform darted back and forth calling out names, following which six or seven people went into the examining rooms. Before long, they emerged from the rooms, and the names of the second batch were called. Only the indigent came here with their illnesses; one after another they entered with furrowed brows and pained faces—cripples on crutches, people with boils on cloth-wrapped legs, tubercular women, blind adults with white cloth bound around their eyes, blind children with white cloth bound around their eyes, children with boils on their heads. An elderly Russian woman was sitting across from me. Her eyes were closed and she was resting her head against the back of the bench, seemingly asleep. But her mouth kept contracting, and her babushka, which was tied under her chin, moved slowly.

A child was bawling loudly in the children's examining room; the Russian woman rushed out of the examining room and called out a Russian name. A moment later, a Chinese came rushing out of the surgical examining room and called out two Chinese names—a cripple and a man with a swollen face walked into the room.

Since I had been the last to arrive, I expected to be the last to be called for examination; I waited until my back and my head both ached.

"Let's go home. We can come back tomorrow." As I rode back in the ricksha, trees lining the street no longer held any fascination for me. What a way to go see a doctor: not only had my symptoms not lessened, but they seemed to have become worse than ever.

I had to go back there because it was free. My name was called during my second visit, and I entered the

124

obstetrics examination room. Although I had had to wait two hours to get in there, I'd finally made it. And since I'd made it inside, it was time to find out how I was going to be treated.

I was led behind a screen, which concealed a short but very wide and very high platform. A couple of forklike objects rose from either side at the far end. I was told to climb up onto the platform. I was more than a little apprehensive at the time—why did they want me to climb up there? Were they going to operate on me?

Since I refused, the heavy-set Russian woman climbed up first to show me that there was nothing to be afraid of—there would be no operation. After she got down, I climbed up and was treated. This particular treatment required no medication: my abdomen was probed a little, first one side, then the other, and this was followed by a question or two; but my Russian was so poor that I didn't understand much of what the doctor was asking me. I did the best I could, and as I left the examination room, the doctor told me to come back the next day to pick up my medication.

But I never went back, for on my way out of the clinic I learned something from one of the more seriously ill patients. He was moaning, the members of his family were weeping, and I thought that he must have been terminally ill. "They won't give you any medicine here," he told me. "They say it's too expensive, so we have to go out and buy it ourselves. Where are we supposed to get the money?"

I had made two trips to the clinic, then had waited two hours to see the doctor. I guess if I'd gone back there twice more and waited another few hours, my illness would eventually have cured itself! Unfortunately, I didn't have that kind of patience.

39

Thirteen Days

"WE'LL be leaving in less than a month. Just think, we're going! So don't act like a baby. I'll come to see you every couple of days or so," Langhua said to me.

Because of my poor health, I was going to stay with a friend for a few days to rest and build up my strength. At first I didn't want to go, but Langhua, whose idea it had been in the first place, insisted upon it. My illness had gotten so bad by then that I had no strength left at all and my joints were swollen and painful. So, on a rainy day, in the company of friends, I went to my friend's house.

The automobile made its way through the slanting rain; it was coming down so hard it looked like a layer of smoke. How could the driver find his way through such a downpour? To my surprise, he speeded up. As we drove through the rain, I felt like I was sitting in a little room. I found that quite intriguing! After we passed through town and had driven almost all the way to the nearest neighboring village, the sensation suddenly came to me that I was courageously entering a battlefield. Since I was so sick, I didn't call out, "What beautiful scenery!" The automobile was bouncing around so much that I had to hold my abdomen tightly. Illness ruins everything.

I went to bed before nine o'clock that night. But I didn't fall asleep right away. We were in the countryside, where a special kind of loneliness overcame me. The night rain was constantly beating against the window; I was covered with sweat, like someone who has just had a terrible nightmare. But then I felt a chill, with the coldness seemingly oozing from my joints; I was like a malaria victim—hot one minute, cold the next!

I felt as though I were about to disintegrate, and I began to cry. But since I had no mother, who would hear me cry?

The next night was the same, and the third. I didn't cry any more—I couldn't. I was like a sick cat. I had to bear my pain alone. For an entire week I sat on the *kang*, my comforter wrapped around me. When I wasn't sitting on the *kang*, I was lying on it.

The plum tree beyond the window had bloomed. I could see the lovely white flowers.

The Autumn Festival was only twenty days away— we would be gone by then.

I watched through the window as the white flowers fell from the plum tree. Small fruits were growing in their place. I was well enough by then to move a chair outside and sit beneath the tree to watch the flowers.

Langhua didn't come over to see me until I had been there eight days. It was almost as though my own father or mother were coming to visit me. I felt so shy when I saw him that I didn't even say hello; all I did was let him sit near me.

I knew as well as anyone that getting sick was a common occurrence. Who didn't get sick once in a while? But I was still unhappy. Even though I didn't shed any tears, the sadness lasted a very long time, as though someone were mistreating me. Such a stormy night, a night of alternating hot and cold, of solitary fantasies.

The second time Langhua came to visit me, I insisted on returning home with him.

"You can't go home. Once you're home, you'll have to start working again, but you're supposed to be taking it easy and getting better. We'll be leaving in less than two weeks. If you try to get up as soon as you're feeling a little better and then wind up getting sick again, there won't be a thing I can do about it."

"Going home. I'm going home."

"Okay, you go home! What can you do with someone who doesn't know how to use her head, someone who can't even control herself? All right, you go home, but if you get sick again, don't come crying to me!"

Once again I was left behind, as the plums on the tree grew bigger and bigger. My thoughts were more confusing than ever. Poor people have no home, so when they get sick, they have to live with friends.

Already it had been thirteen days!

40

Selling Off Our Belongings

WITH heavy hearts we went into the kitchen to take stock of what we had: we would sell our water pitcher, our water bucket, our little pot, and such things. This wasn't the first time I had taken stock. When we had first talked about leaving, I had gone into the kitchen and done some figuring: thirty cents for this, twenty cents for that. I don't know how many times I went through this procedure, but almost every time the word "leave" was mentioned, I would start in with my figuring. Now the time had come to sell the stuff.

The merchant who dealt in used goods was waiting outside the door.

He gave me an estimate of what it was all worth: the water pitcher, the board for making noodles, the water bucket, the ceramic crock, three rice bowls, the soy-sauce bottle, the cooking-oil bottle—he said he'd pay fifty cents for the lot.

We didn't answer—we couldn't sell it for that price.

"Fifty cents is a lot of money for that stuff. Look here, the pot leaks! This is an old water bucket. You could buy it for about a dime. As for the noodle board, even if I do buy it, I won't be able to do anything with it. The rice bowls aren't worth much." He made gestures in the air with one hand, while he examined the things laid out on the floor with the other. He obviously didn't think much of this stuff. "What do you think it's worth? It isn't worth anything."

"If it's not worth anything, then we won't sell it. You'd better leave!"

"The pot leaks! A leaky pot!" He kept tapping the bottom of the pot with his finger, so that one resounding "ping" after another rent the air.

I was concerned that he'd eventually knock the bottom right off the pot. I didn't want to part with it like that. "We're not selling it. You'd better leave!"

"Look, this stuff is a bunch of junk. Even if I do buy it from you, I'll have trouble selling it."

"I cook with it every day," I said, "so how could it leak?"

"You say it doesn't leak, but I can see it with my own eyes. Just feel how thin the bottom is." He gave the bottom two final taps, almost longingly.

The next morning I used that same little pot to cook rice for breakfast—it would be the last time. That made me very sad: tomorrow it was going to leave us and go to the house of someone else! *I'll never see it again, this little pot of ours.* When there was no rice in the house, we had filled it with water to boil for drinking, and when there was just a little rice, we had made rice gruel in it. Now it was going to leave us!

The little pot that had shared our misfortunes, was it sad that it was going to leave us?

We sold our old comforter, our old shoes, our old socks, all of it.

Then there was the sword; when I mentioned selling it, Langhua said. "Let's give it to my student! It's not a good idea to sell it, since my name is carved on it."

The day before, his student had heard that he was leaving and had cried.

It was right in the middle of their martial arts lesson. The student had stood there, sword in hand, while tears ran down his face.

41

The Final Week

WE walked down the street, which was still wet after the rainfall that had just ended. We hesitated when we reached Central Avenue: should we go over to the river? If not, where should we go? Clouds were still in the sky, and few people were out on the street. We weren't walking anywhere in particular, but we couldn't just keep walking.

"Langhua, we ought to fix a date. What day should we leave?"

"Today's the third, so let''s go on the thirteenth. Ten days. What do you say?"

I stopped in my tracks. That really brought me up short. We were actually going to leave Harbin! In only ten days. After that, we would pass our days on trains or on the open sea, and we'd no longer be able to see the Sungari. As long as there was a "Manchukuo," we would never again set foot on this soil.

Li and Chen Cheng dropped by; the general feeling was that we had made the right decision.

"Only seven days to go. You're smart to leave!" Chen Cheng said.

Lao Zhang invited us to dinner to celebrate our impending departure. When dinner was over, we all went for a stroll in the park. We bought some ice cream, but no matter what we did, nothing seemed the same. The tall trees, the summer winds, the sand, the flowers and grass, the pond, the man-made hill, the open-air arbor on top of the hill—everything seemed different. And I was different; I no longer ran around the park, carefree as could be. I walked along with measured steps as the sand crunched noisily beneath my feet.

I was left all alone at night in our room. Wang Yuxiang came over and looked at me through the window; he paced back and forth outside, pretending that he wasn't really interested in watching me but was just passing the time. He kept looking at everything in the room, and when that no longer satisfied him, he asked me, "Where did my teacher go?"

"Why do you want him?"

"I want to take my lesson."

Actually, the boy was seldom all that interested in taking his lesson. What intrigued him now was the sense that something was going on here. Otherwise, why would we have sold all those things over the past few days? Used cotton wadding, a tattered leather mat . . .

They're going to move! The boy couldn't figure out exactly what was amiss. He ran home to call Xiao Ju over. The girl was the same age as he, so naturally she also sensed that something was happening. I turned off the lamp. Even though I wanted to take care of some things, I didn't dare do it right then.

I lay down on the bed and felt the wall with my hand, then I felt the bed; I still had contact with these things, but in seven days I would be leaving them all.

In the end, the little pot and the water pitcher were taken away by the dealer in used goods; they clanked in his hand as he carried them off, the sun's rays glinting from them as they disappeared through the gate. Langhua had bought them the winter before at a flea market. Now they were going back to the same place.

My sadness at selling the water pitcher was even harder to bear. Then, on legs that didn't seem to belong to me, I walked out to the woodshed, where I noticed that many pieces of unburned firewood remained; should we sell it? Give it to friends? An electric heater stood behind the house, also a pair of worn-out shoes.

The stove had lost its companions, the pot and the water pitcher. The kitchen didn't look like a kitchen any more.

Four days of our final week had passed, and my mood of distress increased with each passing day. We couldn't cook at home, so we ate out, or at the homes of friends.

Every time I saw someone else's cooking pot, I thought of the one we had sold, and I lost my appetite. I couldn't even enjoy a peaceful sleep.

"They're coming over tomorrow morning at six o'clock to take the bed away, so we have to get up a little earlier."

This remark by Langhua drove home the fact that we would be leaving very soon! That we had to leave! It was almost as though we wouldn't have to leave if he simply wouldn't say anything.

I had a fitful sleep that night. The metal gate rattled before sunrise the following morning. The sound threw a fright into me, as though it were coming to steal my heart away. I sat up in a sort of daze, but Langhua jumped out of bed. Once we were both out of bed, we removed the comforter, the straw mat, and the pillows, and dumped them onto the floor at our feet, almost frenetically. Someone was knocking at the door; the dog was setting up a din in the courtyard.

The sound of horsebells came through the window. This sort of morning was now in our past. We were like people who had just suffered a calamity as we stood in the completely empty room.

I spread the bedding out on the floor and lay down to sleep. After days and days of being sick and ill at ease, I was so weak that I could barely get my body to do my bidding. Langhua went over to the riverbank to wash his shirt; when he returned home and saw that I was not yet up, he said angrily, "It doesn't matter to a lazybones like you what time it is. Get up and get things ready. We should be packing the things that we can carry with us."

"What's there to get ready? I've already done everything. It's still early, and I'm going to get a little more sleep. I didn't sleep all night." My legs were sore, the small of my back ached, and I felt as though I might get sick again.

"If you want to sleep, do it after everything has been taken care of. Now, get up!"

So we rolled up the bedding that was on the floor. Dark spots caused by the smoke from burning candles dotted the four walls from the ceiling all the way down. Our voices echoed slightly in the empty room, and we had all the space to walk around in that we could possibly need.

We ate our last breakfast—bread and sausage.

I held a little bundle in my hand. Langhua said, "Let's go!" He pushed open the door.

When we first moved here, Langhua had said, "Go on in!" I passed through the open door—my legs were trembling, my heart was as heavy as it had ever been, and I couldn't stop the flow of tears. It was the time to cry. My tears had every right to flow.

I walked straight out the gate, without once turning back to take a look. We had left our home! Cars on the street, pedestrians, little shops, poplars lining the sidewalks. We turned the corner!

We had left Market Street.

My little bundle hung limp from my hand. We walked south down Central Avenue.

Afterword

SINCE I appear in this book, I feel I should have the right to pen a few lines here. If the reader feels that my words are superfluous, then I can only say that the very printing of this book is, in itself, superfluous.

How can I say that? This is, purely and simply, a partial record of life, which must be taken at face value. But I love it, and I love it precisely because it must be taken at face value, for something of us is in it. The reader may get something else from it, but that would be more than we had hoped for.

One loves oneself more intimately than one loves others. This love for *oneself* is especially strong when dealing with the details of one's life. That's how I feel.

LANGHUA